Goshen, Maryland

A History and Its People

Ardith Gunderman Boggs

Janet Lee, Editor

HERITAGE BOOKS
2011

HERITAGE BOOKS
AN IMPRINT OF HERITAGE BOOKS, INC.

Books, CDs, and more—Worldwide

For our listing of thousands of titles see our website
at
www.HeritageBooks.com

Published 2011 by
HERITAGE BOOKS, INC.
Publishing Division
100 Railroad Ave. #104
Westminster, Maryland 21157

Copyright © 1994 Ardith Gunderman Boggs

Cover art courtesy of Ardith Gunderman Boggs and Joyce Hawkins

All rights reserved. No part of this book may be reproduced or transmitted in any form or by any means, electronic or mechanical, including photocopying, recording or by any information storage and retrieval system without written permission from the author, except for the inclusion of brief quotations in a review.

International Standard Book Numbers
Paperbound: 978-1-55613-987-1
Clothbound: 978-0-7884-8949-5

DEDICATION

To all those who care about those who came before.

CONTENTS

PREFACE	vii
GOSHEN: FROM THE BEGINNING	1
MAP OF GOSHEN	11
CHESAPEAKE AND OHIO CANAL	17
HONEYSUCKLE HILL (GOSHEN)	21
JONES FAMILY CEMETERY	33
FERTILE MEADOWS	37
SYCAMORE HOLLOW ON WILDCAT CREEK	43
ATWOOD-BLUNT HOME	47
AVALON	49
BLACK AND WHITE INN	53
JOHN SAMUEL DAVIS HOMESTEAD AND MILL	57
DAVIS FAMILY GENEALOGY	61
FOX LAIR	81
GOSHEN MANOR	83
GREEN HILLS FARM	85
SOMERSET ORME JONES FARM	89
OAKHURST	93
OLD GOSHEN METHODIST CHURCH	95
IGNATIUS PIGMAN	101
GOSHEN SCHOOLS	105
PRATHERTOWN	109
HARRISON AND GLADYS KING	111
GOSHEN GHOSTS	115
WINDHAM FARM	119
WOODBOURNE	123

Preface

LAND OF GOSHEN

*We're in the Land of Goshen, where the trees grow strong and tall,
where the north wind blows on all it knows,
and the crows from the tree-tops call.*

Land of Goshen ...

*We live in the Land of Goshen, where the turf is soft and green,
where the sunrise creeps to a vibrant red,
and its rays from the blue sky beam.*

Land of Goshen ...

*We're in the Land of Goshen, where the gentle hills call my name,
where the riders mount their mighty steeds, to hunt for their fox in vain.*

Land of Goshen ...

*I love the Land of Goshen, but I dream of a fragrant spring, for the cold winter snows blanket all that grows,
while children's voices from the valleys ring.*

Land of Goshen ...

Land of Goshen ...

Ardith Gunderman Boggs, 1972

AUTHOR'S NOTE

I am deeply appreciative to all the people who were willing to share with me their memories of Goshen. In so many cases their memories included stories told to them by their ancestors, stories that would eventually be lost if it were not for the written page. Many, over the years, have encouraged me to continue compiling the history of Goshen. My dream is now a reality. My book about this lovely place, Goshen, is finished. I regret that I was not able to include all the fine people who lived and died here, each shaping the community in his or her own special way. But this book is in THEIR honour, and has accomplished my goal. My biggest joy, however, has been talking to the Goshen people who, as their ancestors before them, love this place....

I am indebted to a very special friend, Janet Lee, who has been my editor and proof reader. She always seemed to delight in receiving another chapter to scrutinize. Without her able assistance, this book would probably never have happened.

Much effort has been made to verify the authenticity of the material. However, since some of these writings are based on recalled memories, I recognize there could be inaccuracies. I would appreciate any readers bringing additional materials or discrepancies to my attention.

To those of you who will read this book, I ask that you join me in helping to make sure that Goshen's future will be guided by those who insist on holding hands with the past.

GOSHEN: FROM THE BEGINNING

This community of Goshen, originally part of Saint Mary's County and Prince Georges County, became Frederick County in 1748, and in 1776 became Montgomery County.

In 1743, a land grant, consisting of Benjamin's Square and Land of Goshen, was deeded to Benjamin Wallingford. At this time log cabins were scattered here and there, housing the early settlers.

Sometime after 1737, the Pigman family bought quantities of land and started several mills. By 1790, records indicated two mills, a copper mine, mill dams and races, and a log cabin used for a mill store on property referred to as Pigman's Purchase.

This valley was indeed the land of milk and honey; fertile, just perfect for growing tobacco and corn. Early in the 1800's attention was turned to growing wheat.

A system of high hills known as Parr's Ridge crosses the county diagonally. These hills and plateaus are separated by streams and creeks that water the territory abundantly. Seneca Creek is fed by numerous tributaries bordering Parr's Ridge, which is separated from the headwaters of the Patuxent River by a barrier of slate that curves from Damascus to Laytonsville and beyond. One of these tributaries is the Goshen Branch, sometimes referred to as Little Seneca, Magruder Creek or Riggs Creek. It is on this creek, along Goshen Road (now Brink), where the mills were built that became the backbone of the early farming community of "Goshen Mills." By 1845, the name was simply "Goshen."

Land records of Montgomery County indicate that Joshua Pigman built a home overlooking the mills in 1792. However, that same year he sold parts of Pigman's Purchase and the resurvey of Benjamin's Square to his brother Reverend Ignatius Pigman. The deed makes mention of "premises and improvements." The mills were called Pigman's Mills after the owner and changed names frequently over the years. They were referred to as Crow's Mill in 1794 according to "Early Settlers of Montgomery County & Maps" by Dennis Griffith. Indeed, Ed Crow, a landowner of the day, apparently began buying and selling parts of the above land grants over a period of the next eight years. In 1795 the following ad for Goshen Mills appeared in the January 1, Maryland Journal:

> "Valuable Mills for sale ... Goshen Mills in Montgomery ... on the waters of the Seneca -- on public road that leads from the Mouth of Monocacy to Baltimore town which is

Goshen: From the Beginning

> 35 miles distance and about 27 miles from Georgetown or the Federal City ... the mill seat has 36 feet head and fall which is so calculated as to use that water a second time; there being two mill-houses, one above the other, viz. a brick house three stories high, 36 feet by 25 almost new, the other a framed house 24 feet square, the whole intended to work four pair of stones, three of which are now running, (two burrs, the other cullens) with excellent boulting cloths, etc. for merchant work. There is also materials for a saw-mill, which might be set to work with a trifling expense. About 150 acres of good farming land may be had with the mills, 30 acres of which are rich meadow land ... on this tract of land, (it is generally supposed) there is a rich copper mine ... dwelling ... millers house."
> Ed Crow Nov. 30   Maryland Journal, Jan. 1, 1795

A record of one of the transactions in a deed to Crow from Pigman in 1796 made the following references: "all houses, out houses, edifices, buildings, orchards, garden lands, meadows, commons, pastures, feedings, woods, underwoods, ways, paths, water, watercourses, easements, profits, and commodities and advantages." By 1797, he owned land grants referred to as Land O Goshen, Benjamin Square, Pigmans Purchase, and Fertile Meadows.

During this time in Goshen history, there grew an elm tree in the low-lying area across from the Goshen Store, which, as I write this, is the home of Merle and Roger Young. In those days the store had a sloping front yard that extended down to the road-bed that passed closer to the elm tree. Under its spreading branches, the community gathered to listen to politicians and to discuss the issues of the day. The tree soon became called the "Politicians Tree" or the "Meeting Tree." Today this tree has vanished from the landscape, presumably because of Dutch elm disease. It was partially dead in 1974 and ten years later was completely gone. Fortunately, an oil painting was done of this grand old tree in 1972.

The tree stood proudly in the 1780's and 90's as it witnessed the voters choose Federalist electors in presidential campaigns, saw people favor first George Washington in 1789, and then John Adams in 1797. Thomas Jefferson served as Vice President under John Adams from 1797-1801. As public opinion began to shift, many people in Montgomery County felt that Alexander Hamilton and other Federalists made too many concessions to Britain. This resulted in the growth of an anti-Federalist movement that gradually turned to Thomas Jefferson as their natural leader. However it is important to note that most of Montgomery County remained loyal to the Federalist leaders.

By 1798, Maryland's General Assembly created election districts. The first district in Montgomery County was later called Cracklin District, but had its polling place at Goshen Mills. Thomas Davis was

Goshen: From the Beginning

named election commissioner in 1799. In 1800, the voters of Montgomery County were struck with horror when they realized there was a possibility that Jefferson would be elected president. This led to one of the bitterest campaigns in the history of the county. The vote taken at Goshen Mills (Cracklin District) brought in 154 votes for the Federalists, 52 for the Democratic-Republicans. Over all the states, Jefferson and Aaron Burr had equal electoral college votes, so the House of Representatives voted and Jefferson won with Aaron Burr serving as his Vice President.

When Ed Crow purchased the previously-mentioned land grants a log cabin stood on the site of the Goshen store. This probably was built by the previous owners, the Pigmans. It is unclear how early this structure served as a store or if it also served as a miller's residence. But under the ownership of Crow, it was used as a store in the 1790's. He added on the present kitchen part with the loft, or upper store, being used as an inn or boarding house. An 1800 survey showed a frame house on a hill, smoke houses and storehouses, blacksmith and copper shops, log homes, two Goshen mills and a store/inn.

In 1803, Ed Crow sold 150 acres of land called Fertile Meadows to Sam Robertson and his wife Rachael. The deed makes mention of tenements, mill dam, race, and premises. Just six years earlier Crow had purchased this same 150 acres for 125 pounds sterling, and later built a home or perhaps just added on to the existing structure that was the mill owner's dwelling. The Robertsons were wealthy people from the Annapolis area who wanted to make a fortune in grain. In 1809, Sam Robertson acquired additional tracts of land from Sam Howard and Josiah and Amos Wellcoxen and others. Tracts mention premises and building improvements. Around 1816, Robertson's will declared that the property, including the millrace, be sold for $15,000.00 to pay his debts. He owned 300 acres at this time. He is believed to have died around 1815. The Robertsons had three daughters: Susan (Dorsey), Eliza, and Lydia (Howard). Rachael requested in her will that their Goshen graveyard be decently endorsed and suitable tombstones be placed at the grave of each, the expense of which shall be paid out of the estate at large. She makes reference to husband and several children who are buried there. She died about 1853. They are buried on the Fertile Meadows farm with stones as the proof.

On July 24, 1817, George Washington Riggs of Baltimore purchased from the trustees representing the Robertson estate at public sale, the above mentioned tracts of land for $13,115.00. Rachael Robertson willingly relinquished her claim after receiving purchase money awarded her by the trustees. G. W. Riggs was a well-to-do gentleman who was said to have been a silversmith and lived in Georgetown. He made a great deal of his money in the import and export business. He also owned property in what is now the Baltimore Harbour area. His grand home titled "Woodville" was located outside of the city. He lived there in later years. In 1820 he returned home to run his store,

Goshen: From the Beginning

thus leaving the mills in the hands of Remus D. Riggs. George Washington Riggs was the brother of Elijah Riggs who was founder of the Riggs Bank.

The 1850 survey listed the following: a brick mill several stories tall to mill grain for sale, a frame country mill to grind corn and buckwheat for farmers, an open saw mill, a brick church, a school house, blacksmithies, a store and many homes and farms. This same year the Goshen store added its newest addition. The property was then sold to Michael L. Peugh (Pugh) on May 3, 1851, from his brother-in-law Lloyd Magill. Lloyd Magill's father Basal had purchased this property from G. W. Riggs in 1829 and 1835.

On February 3, 1853 the Goshen Post Office was established. Its location was to be the Goshen Store with Michael Peugh appointed as the first postmaster. A year later, his wife took over as postmistress when her husband died. About 11 different people served as postmasters over the next fifty years. The last postmaster listed was Howard H. Kinsey. The year was 1905. Because of declining commerce in the Goshen community, the post office was then moved to Laytonsville. The following year the property was sold to Margaret Kinsey by Asbury R. Martin. In 1923 the store and property was sold to Annie Prather and husband Rezin. Annie, who was black, was a well-known midwife who assisted Dr. George Boyer of Damascus. Annie also ran the store selling candy, stamps and other items for the convenience of the community. It is said that she also ran the store as a inn and boarding house. There are partition marks on the ceilings in the bedrooms and loft to substantiate this claim. In 1940, the property sold at auction for $800.00 to Brita and Lee Councilman. During this ownership it was an antique shop and precinct headquarters for the Eisenhower/Nixon campaign. In 1966 it sold to the Donald Freeman Family. They removed the square front porch. The Roger Young family purchased it in 1973 and have done much restoration and improvements to the interior, exterior, and grounds. A brick floor replaced the wooden floor in the kitchen, rechinking of the interior and exterior chimneys was done, and aluminum siding has replaced the deteriorating wooden siding. The home is tastefully furnished with antiques.

Remus D. Riggs inherited the Goshen mills in 1859. At this time the Goshen mill complex was dominated by the brick, three story merchant mill which ground wheat into wheat flour for market. The mill had two water wheels driven by double sets of wheels. The frame country mill which ground corn and grain for the farmers, special orders, and feed for cattle, sat on a stone foundation. The saw mill had open sides with the roof on posts. There were store houses and other merchant structures as well. The Riggs family had this property until 1916. Even though they owned the complex, they hired a miller to operate the mills. One such miller was John Davis who was employed from about 1860 to 1879. There was a destructive flood in Montgomery County in 1868 that damaged or destroyed most of the existing mills.

Goshen: From the Beginning

Because one of the Goshen mills was built of brick it survived. No doubt there was extensive damage and much had to be rebuilt. This great mill was said to have a turbine wheel and 42" stones all bound in iron. It needed two streams to furnish enough water to make it operate.

Sometime in the early 1880's, John Davis either leased or began to purchase his own mill from Washington D. Waters. This deed for sale was executed in 1885 for $4000.00: 136 and 1/2 acres of Benjamin Square, Brook Grove, Mill Pond, Thomas Hog Pasture, and Dublin, in the area of what is now called Davis Mill Road. The ownership of this mill and property can be traced back from W. D. Waters to his father Dr. Washington Waters, to Elisha Owen Williams who inherited it from his mother Mary Dorsey Williams Waters. Elisha was a half brother to Washington Waters. Mary in turn inherited the mill and property from her father, Harry (sometimes listed as Henry) W. Dorsey, who purchased it from the family of Charles Greenbury Griffith. At the time of the Griffith ownership, a 1783 Maryland tax assessment record gave considerable detail of the improvements to this property. It consisted of 364 acres with a dwelling consisting of two rooms and an entry on the lower floor, a charnel, log kitchen, corn house, stables and barn, and a grist mill on a good stream of water. There were many out buildings as well. Before the Griffith ownership, Lodowick Davis, a carpenter, owned part of this property after purchasing it from Benjamin Wollingsford in 1754.

Davis built a home on the hill across from the mill on Blunt Road. His wife's name was Mary Ellen, and together they had fourteen children.

In 1880, Charles T. Edmonston was also one of the millers at the Goshen Mills complex. On August 27, 1890, a sudden and mysterious fire destroyed the mills and the miller's house. Passing neighbors awoke the family which saved their lives. G. W. Moxley was miller at the time of the fire. The loss was estimated at $5000.00. By the late 1800's there was much competition between mills, as newer and more modern mills were operational in Gaithersburg and other towns. Some of the new mills were steam-powered. It is not surprising that some of these were thought to have been purposely set on fire. By this time the Goshen mills, now referred to as the Riggs mills, were becoming shabby and worn. They would have probably closed down even if the fire had not occurred.

No community is complete without a church, and Goshen is no exception. Ignatius Pigman sold a plot of land for 5 shillings to the local Methodists who built a little log church on the site sometime before 1788. The deed was formalized in 1790. The little log church was often referred to as Pigman's Chapel and later as Goshen Chapel. However, in later years it has been lovingly called "Old Goshen." A very complete history of "Old Goshen" was written by Ella Plummer and published by the Montgomery County Historical Society in November of

Goshen: From the Beginning

1962 (a later chapter).

Richard Waters Jr., son of Dr. Richard Waters of Revolutionary war fame, taught school in the log church. He was known as "Uncle Dickey" and lived to be over ninety years of age. He joined the church later in life but was said to be of great inspiration to the minister. With his wisdom gained from a long, full life, he must have been an inspiration to the children as well. A second Goshen school called South Public School was located on the corner of Route 124 and Brink Road. When the children arrived at school one morning, they found the school nearly burned to the ground.

Harry Riggs generously donated an acre of land for $50.00 for the third Goshen school. This was a little one room schoolhouse built on what was then Blunt Road. Today the road has been renamed Huntmaster. The little schoolhouse is the center section of a former tenant house that belonged to the Green Hills Dairy Farm, operated by the Stiles family until the property was sold in 1987 for development. The schoolhouse is located just down the hill, on the right, a short distance from the Goshen School Road intersection.

Green Hills farm had been in the Riggs family for five generations. The last owners were the four daughters of R. D. Riggs. One of them, Barbara Riggs Stiles, rented the farm and lived there with her husband and family. They operated the dairy farm for many years. R. D. Riggs' father was Harry Riggs, and Harry's father was Remis Dorsey Riggs. He was the son of George Washington Riggs. The little school was used until 1919 when children were then hauled in horse-drawn wagons to Laytonsville, where the new school had been built. In 1989, a beautiful new Goshen School for area children was opened and is located on Miracle Drive in Goshen Estates.

Many of the original homes that still remain in the Goshen area have been beautifully restored. Some are on the Historical Registry. Listed below are some historical homes and other sites of interest in Goshen:
"Fertile Meadows"
Old Post Office and Store
"Honeysuckle Hill" (formerly "Goshen")
Jones Family Graveyard
Somerset Orme Jones Farm (later called Judge Chambers Farm)
Black and White Inn
"Goshen Manor"
"Old Goshen" Methodist (presently Mennonite) Church
Brick House
The King Farm
Goshen School on Huntmaster Road
Green Hills Farm House
"Avalon"
Atwood Blunt Home - razed by the fire department in the 1990's

Goshen: From the Beginning

"Fox Lair" (originally "Locust Grove")
"Oakhurst"
John Davis Homestead ruins and old mill foundations
"Woodbourne"
Windham Farm
"Sycamore Hollow"
Warfield Home
Wightman Farm

Goshen: From the Beginning

Gladys King History, Goshen Homemakers Club

Gladys King Oral History

Harrison King Oral History

Mary Burton, Sycamore Hollow and Wildcat Creek

History of Goshen Mills and Immediate Area by The Goshen Mills Chapter, National Society DAR

Post Office Department, Washington DC

Goshen Mills Post Office and Store, Ardie Boggs for Sugarloaf Foundation, MCHS

History of Early Water Mills in Montgomery County by Eleanor M. V. Cook

Woodbourne Quilt, MCHS

Goshen Walking Tour Notes, Ardie Boggs, MCHS

Riggs Family Oral Histories

Maryland Journal, January 1, 1795, MCHS

Self

Photo by Sarah Greenhalgh

The old Goshen post office/store is now a private residence and was once an important gathering place in the town of Goshen. The present-day dining room was originally a log cabin built in the 1700s.

Goshen Mill once more than hunt country

By David Sutton

Long before "Goshen" became synonymous with exclusive hunt country acreage, it was a small but booming mill settlement.

Newspaper accounts from the 1850s indicate an extensive community centered on wood and grain mills on Brink Road (formerly Goshen).

Courtesy of The Gaithersburg Gazette

Goshen: From the Beginning

KEY:

1. Old Goshen Methodist Church
2. Fertile Meadows (mill owner's home)
3. Mill Sites
4. Goshen Post Office and Store
5. Somerset Orme Jones farm
6. Black and White Inn
7. Warfield farm
8. Wightman farm
9. Honeysuckle Hill ("Goshen")
10. Brick House (Chas. F. Hogan is shown, on original map, as owner in 1879. He was a blacksmith.)
11. Green Hills farm (Riggs)
12. Goshen Schoolhouse
13. Harrison King farm
14. Atwood-Blunt home site
15. Avalon
16. Fox Lair
17. Oakhurst
18. Davis Mill site
19. Davis home site
20. Sycamore Hollow
21. Woodbourne
22. South Public School location
23. Windham farm
24. Goshen Manor

Goshen: From the Beginning

This map was taken from an 1879 Atlas by Hopkins of Montgomery County. New roads and changed road names have been added to make it easier to read. Many roadbeds have been changed since this map was printed.

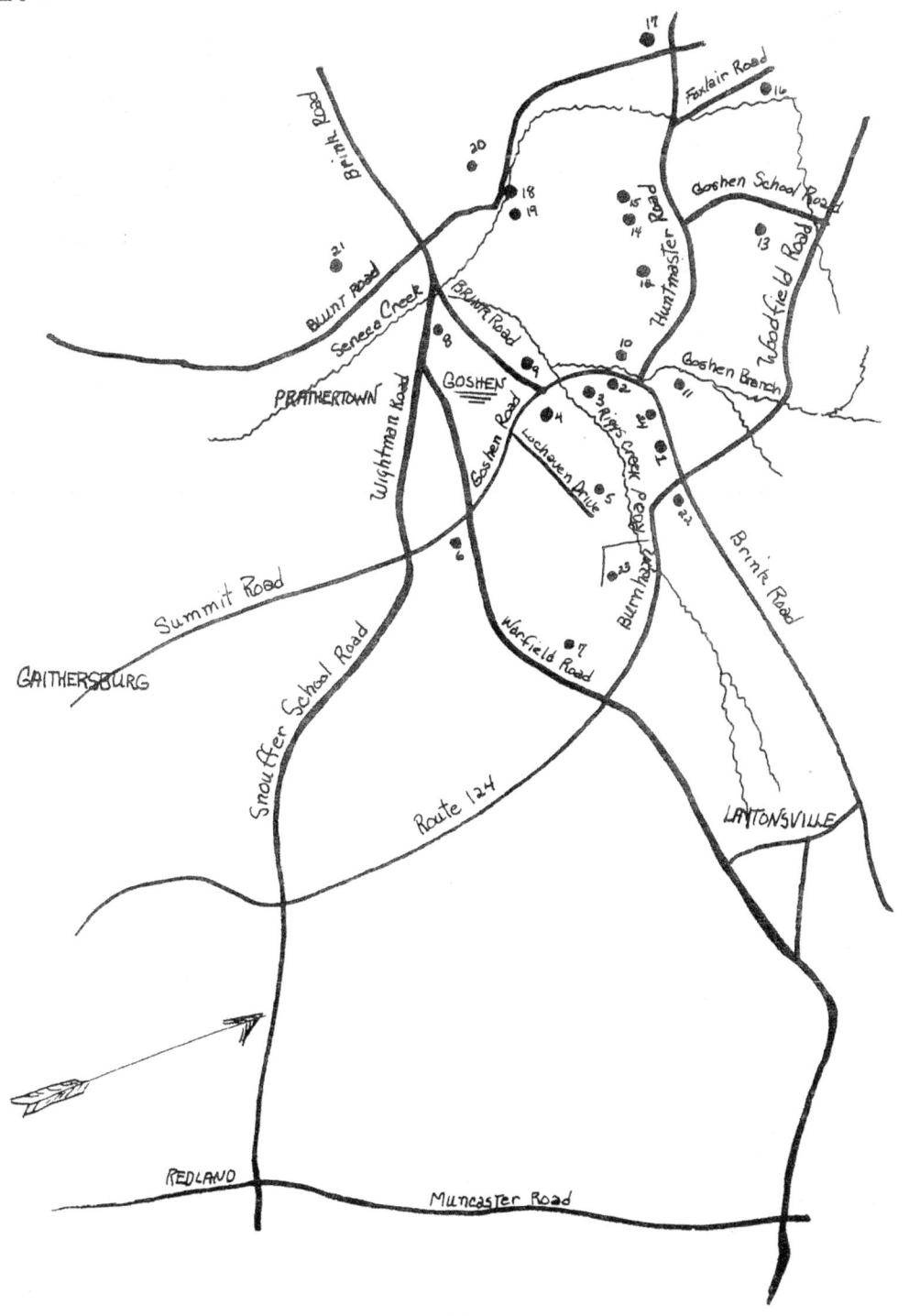

Goshen Post Office and Store as Eisenhower and Nixon Headquarters

Courtesy of Ardith Gunderman Boggs

Goshen: From the Beginning

GOSHEN POST OFFICE, MONTGOMERY COUNTY, MARYLAND

ESTABLISHED: FEBRUARY 3, 1853
DISCONTINUED: NOVEMBER 15, 1905

POSTMASTERS   APPOINTMENT DATES 1883 - 1971

Michael L. Peugh   February 3, 1853
Henrietta D. Peugh   September 22, 1854
John L. Brown   September 11, 1857
Robert A. McPherson   September 15, 1859
Richard Jones   November 26, 1861
Nathan C. Dickerson   March 8, 1866
Charles T. Edmonston   March 18, 1880
Asbury R. Martin   November 20, 1882
McClellan Thompson   May 26, 1894
Howard H. Kinsey   December 21, 1895

Courtesy of Joyce Hawkins

Merle Young, owner of Goshen Post Office & Store turned residence

Post Office Department, Washington, DC

self

Goshen: From the Beginning

GOSHEN DIRECTORY: 1879

Population 50, one church; Methodist Episcopal, South Public School, and two mills

Postmaster,
    Martin, A. R.

Blacksmith,
    Hogan, C. F.

Merchandise,
    Martin, A. R.

Millers,
    Davis, J. S.
    Lewis, J. W.

Farmers,
    Benson, J. E.
    Blunt, W. W.
    Bowman, Uriah G.
    Dorsey, R. G.
    Green, Richard
    Higgins, James
    Higgins, Thomas
    Jones, Richard W.
    Jones, Somerset
    La Mar, J. C.
    Magruder, H. R.
    Magruder, J. S.
    Magruder, Wm. M.
    Magruder, Z. M.
    McMahan, E.
    Merriweather, A. G.
    Miller, Washington
    Reed, William
    Riggs, George
    Riggs, R. D.
    Riggs, Harry
    Stewart, A. G.
    Thompson, J. H.
    Thompson, J. C.
    Thompson, William of C
    Waters, J. McC
    Waters, W. D

Courtesy of Ardith Gunderman Boggs

History of Montgomery County Maryland by T. H. S. Boyd, Montgomery County Historical Society

GOSHEN DIRECTORY: 1880

Population 40, Methodist Episcopal Church, public and private schools near

Postmaster,
    Martin, A. R.

Blacksmith,
    Campbell, James

Millers,
    Davis, J. S.
    Edmonston, O. T.

General Merchandise,
    Pumphry, R. H.   Pumphry moved his store to Germantown in October 14, 1881

Pianos and Organs,
    Waters, W. D.

Courtesy of Ardith Gunderman Boggs   *Politician's Tree*

The Maryland Directory; Baltimore, Maryland Steamship Company Montgomery County Historical Society

People and Places and Pot Pourri by Jacobs Malloy, Montgomery County Historical Society

Goshen : From the beginning

GOSHEN DIRECTORY: 1882

Postmaster,
    Martin, A. R.

Blacksmiths,
    Barber and Scheckles

Millers,
    Davis, J. S.
    Edmonston, O. T.

Merchandiser,
    Pumphry, R. H.

Music,
    Sipe, Thomas A.

Fertilizers,
    Waters, W. D. & Sons

Courtesy of Ardith Gunderman Boggs

1882 Maryland Directory, MCHS

Chesapeake and Ohio Canal

CHESAPEAKE AND OHIO CANAL

Before the end of the Revolutionary War, George Washington realized the promise of the Western Maryland and beyond. The region was rich in timber, furs, and lands for agriculture. In 1785, he became the first president of the Patowmack Company which was chartered both in Virginia and Maryland to make the Potomac River navigable from tidewater to the western limits, and to improve the tributaries for navigation. A chain of locks and canals that skirted around rapids at Little Falls, Great Falls, Seneca and Harpers Ferry was completed by 1802. This made it possible for 218 miles of the river to be used for navigation. When New York State began work on the Erie Canal in 1817, it became obvious to the people of Maryland and Virginia that a navigable canal, independent of the river, was needed to provide a direct water communication between the Potomac River and Ohio River Valleys. Overland shipping costs were prohibitive because of poor road systems, length of time taken to get goods to the various markets, and the frequency of breakdowns, etc. In 1828, Virginia, Maryland and Pennsylvania chartered the Chesapeake and Ohio Canal Company. Work began on July 4th of that year. The canal opened to Seneca in 1831, to Harpers Ferry in 1834, to the Cacapon River above Hancock in 1839, and to Cumberland in 1850. Here it stopped forever, having a cost of over $11,000,000. During it's construction, the canal was plagued by labor shortages, unrest, illness, unavailable construction materials, short-lived federal support, constant shortages of funds, unforeseen problems due to geography, and legal battles with the new Baltimore and Ohio Railroad, which started the very same day in July, 1828.

For the people of Goshen in Montgomery County, the canal brought prosperity. The farmers were able to gain access to the much-needed nutrients for their exhausted fields. The canal brought in guano, lime and plaster to fertilize and condition the soil. They gained access to a wider market, because they could load their crops on the barges at a nearby lock, and send their goods to the Port of Georgetown and beyond. Crops could be stored in warehouses at Georgetown until prices were better. Mills sprang up along the canal and by streams throughout the county because the markets for grain and lumber were beyond expectation. People were needed to tend the locks on the canal as well as for operating the barges. The canal reached its height of prosperity in the 1870s. After the devastation caused by the 1889 flood, the canal went into a receivership to the B&O Railroad. It operated until a second flood in 1924 when it was closed down forever.

Today the canal and its towpath, with beautiful bordering forests and flowers, and river landscapes, attract thousands of nature lovers

Chesapeake and Ohio Canal

each year. It will be forever preserved for mankind.

Courtesy of Ardith Gunderman Boggs

Chesapeake and Ohio Canal

Chesapeake and Ohio Canal, Handbook 142, Division of Publications, National Park Service, U.S. Department of the Interior, Washington, D.C. 1991

Self

Honeysuckle Hill ("Goshen")

HONEYSUCKLE HILL
("GOSHEN")

This home is 19th century; it was built by John Jones and his family about 1820. John Jones married a neighbor, Anne Smith Waters, and they had at least ten children. The home later passed down to John Jones' son Richard. After Richard's death, the grown children who remained on the farm were: Priscilla, Margaret, Somerset, Sarah Emma, and her husband Capt. Reuben Riggs. Emma, who didn't marry until her seventies, was the youngest of John Jones' children. She was famous for her butter that was sold to the well-to-do in Washington, D.C. Her husband Reuben, who was a widower at the time of their marriage, was often referred to as Mr. Jones. Emma lived there until her death in 1929, and was the last to be buried in the Jones family graveyard by their home. In the years that followed, the home remainded vacant for some eleven years and then became a tenant farm. During this time, hogs were kept in the parlor and chickens in an upstairs bedroom. An annex was added about 1950.

The following memories, edited for ease in reading, were written by the great-granddaughter of John Jones, Katherine Riggs Poole, in November, 1969.

("GOSHEN")

"In the early eighteen hundreds, a severe epidemic raged along the Potomac River where Evan Jones and his wife, Mary O'Neale, lived near what is now Potomac. Several of their children died, and the parents wished to move their remaining children to a healthier location. Lands were bought near the headwaters of Seneca, and John Jones, Evan, William and Priscilla moved there while the parents remained in the old home.

"In a few years, John married a neighbor, Anne Smith Waters, and set up housekeeping in the house we all know as "Goshen." His brother William died quite young. Uncle Evan (pronounced Ivven in the Welsh manner) and Aunt Prissie lived in what was later known as "Uncle Som's place" and still later the "Chambers place." John and Anne's children were: Mary Ellen, Evan Aquilla, Richard, Margaret, William, Priscilla, Elizabeth, Eugene, Somerset, and Emma. Mary Ellen married Lloyd Linthicum; Evan Aquilla married Rachel Riggs; William died young; Elizabeth became the wife of her first cousin William T. Jones; Eugene went into business in Baltimore, married Emily Walsh and died quite young. Richard, Margaret, Priscilla, Somerset and Emma remained at home. When Emma married Reuben Riggs (a widower) later in life, he moved to "Goshen" with her.

Honeysuckle Hill ("Goshen")

"Margaret (Aunt Mag) was the dominant one of the family. Well educated, with a strong sense of family pride and upright character, she instilled respect and affection in all who came in contact with her. Although she died long before I was born, her presence always seemed a part of "Goshen."

"My first recollection of "Goshen" was a visit to see Uncle Dick who was in his last illness. He was occupying the room which afterwards was Aunt Emma's. Martha and I, who were told to go in and speak to him, approached the footboard of the walnut bed, above which our heads barely reached, and said in unison, "Uncle Dick, we're sorry you're sick."

"After that, Aunt Pris, Uncle Som, Aunt Emma and Uncle Reuben were the inhabitants of "Goshen," about whom my own personal recollections center. Aunt Pris was tall and erect with snow-white hair, which she twisted into a knot on the back of her head, and fastened with a small ebony comb. She usually wore neat dresses of gray-printed cotton, well starched, except on Sunday when she dressed in her best black to go to church. She arose very early, soon after the farm bell was rung about daylight (I have always wondered who rang the bell). As we usually slept in the other bed in her room, I used to open one eye to watch her dress "underneath her nightgown" and emerge in a long muslin chemise from neck to heels before putting on her dress. I don't know why she had to unlock everything and see that there was no waste in preparing breakfast for the hands as well as the household. She also took charge of the poultry. I can remember the different ways she had of calling the different types: Chickoo-chickee for the chickens, peep-peep-pee for the turkeys, and widdy-widdy-widdy for the ducks. Around the pump in the back yard where she fed the poultry, the criss-cross tracks of the turkeys in the soft mud where the trough over-flowed, always reminded me of the network of wrinkles in her face. Another characteristic I remember in connection with her was her habit of taking a coffee break (or perhaps it was tea) in mid-morning. She would bring her cup out on the porch, sit in a rocker, and support the elbow of her "drinking arm" with her other hand while she sipped.

"Uncle Som, also tall, thin, and erect with white hair and beard, was most distinguished looking. When the old people on the other farm died, he bought out the other heirs; from then on, farming this place, which he called Kildeer Park, was his occupation. He continued to live at home, putting a tenant into the house but he went over every day to see what was going on. He had his own horse and buggy. Each morning he would call through a megaphone from the porch to the stable directly across the road from the house and give instructions to have his horse saddled or hitched up to the buggy and brought into the yard where it was tied to an iron ring in a cedar tree on the drive, to await his pleasure. He was a true gentleman farmer. No one ever saw him work, and he was always well dressed and immaculate. He had his suits tailored in Washington and even in summer was never seen without

Honeysuckle Hill ("Goshen")

a coat and tie. After each meal, he would carry out scraps from the table to feed his dogs, Setter and Pointer. In his gentle mellow voice he called "dorgie, dorgie", until they appeared. In his youth he had been attentive to various ladies, but it was said he was too timid to ever propose and so remained a bachelor. He had served two terms in the State Legislature and was always interested in politics.

"Now we come to Aunt Emma who was a most colorful and interesting individual. The youngest of the family, she had been the spoiled darling both at her own home and in that of her uncle, Dr. William Jones in Washington where she visited frequently. He was prominent in society in the Capital where he was City Postmaster and friend and physician to President Buchanan and other leading families. Aunt Emma enjoyed the opportunity of mingling with the best of city society. However, her stern Methodist upbringing prevented her from dancing, card playing, theater, and such worldly pursuits. In addition, her affections were fixed upon a country neighbor, Washington Griffith, who was a clerk in the Riggs Bank in Washington. In later years she would say that he was "over Charlie Glover" (who later became President of Riggs), and had he lived he would probably have been president of the bank. However, he died in his early twenties and Aunt Emma was heartbroken. She wanted to marry "Wash" on his death bed, but her family disapproved, so she wore the wide gold band, intended for the wedding, on her ring finger even after she married Uncle Reuben, placing his wedding ring above it so that the two rings came up to her knuckle. The enlarged crayon portrait of her young lover also hung over her bed through the rest of her life. She had her lover's hair made into a brooch and two earrings with solid gold mountings, which were her only jewelry. After Wash's death and the changes brought about by the Civil War, she devoted her energies to making money. She bought more dairy cows and started making butter to ship to Washington to sell at sixty cents a pound to wealthy customers. Since there was no refrigeration then, and the trip to Washington took several hours, there were some complaints of the butter being strong, but she did very well with the business. When her brother Richard died, she took over the management of Goshen Farm and kept her watchful eye over every activity, farming with hands instead of by a tenant. She watched the commodity price lists in the Sun Papers as an investor reads the stock market report. She knew just when to sell her crops to the best advantage. When she decided to marry Reuben Riggs it was only on condition that he come to live at "Goshen" and that he have no right of inheritance in her farm or she in his farm which he continued to manage. They were married in the bay window of the parlor of our house in Washington with some florist palms for background. A satin-covered pillow was to kneel on, and Martha and Kitty, in pink organdy dresses with white moire ribbon sashes, were wide-eyed attendants. When father obtained the license for her, she would not give her age saying "over fifty" would be sufficient, but it was more likely over sixty. The ceremony was performed by her niece's husband, the Reverend Henry Hamill of the

Honeysuckle Hill ("Goshen")

southern Methodist Church. From then on until his death in 1910, Uncle Reuben was an interesting member of the Goshen household. He must have had a wonderful disposition to fit so smoothly into the "Jones" idiosyncrasies. I am sure his children thought he was giving up a great deal more than he gained by the arrangement. He, too, was tall, with black hair and a black mustache somewhat stained by tobacco from chewing. I can see him now, taking his pocket knife out to cut a piece from the plug and manipulating the "chaw" around his mouth until it was in proper condition. This habit was one independence he retained; another was going without a coat and tie in hot weather, showing his suspenders and a stiffly starched white shirt, with the collar band fastened by a gold collar button. When "dressed up," he wore a high-standing collar and gray ascot tie. Reuben was a Confederate veteran and had a vast store of tales to tell of the hardships of camp life but, at least to the children, he never spoke of the battles. He had great love and sympathy for the "Lost Cause" and had many books and magazines wherein it "lived in song and story." He was always ready to lend a helping hand to any veteran who needed it. In particular a Mr. Lybrand, a painter, was a special protege. Whenever he needed work, there was always something he could do at "Goshen." All the room walls were done with a high gloss paint and embellished by friezes of free-hand daisies and the like running around below the ceilings. The doors and other woodwork were painted a yellowish brown and "grained" with brush strokes to resemble golden oak, I suppose. All of this detracted from the simple charm of a very old house. In winter when there was no work for him, Mr. Lybrand stayed at "Goshen," and to occupy his time, he made paintings of battle scenes. These were quite interesting. They were set in deep frames with the bottom arranged with sand, rocks, etc. to look like the ground. Cutouts of men, flags, guns, etc. were set forward at intervals. When glassed in, with a few additions painted on the glass itself, they gave an appearance of depth, like some modern museum displays. As these works of art increased in number through the years and few were sold, they were rather overpowering and added to the already cluttered appearance of the house.

"Goshen House" was approached through a wide gate from the middle of a very steep road, and the abrupt turn required great skill from the driver of the carriage. The white-fenced front yard was just the width of the long house and contained large trees and shrubs. The circular driveway and walk to the porch were of white gravel from which no wood or blade of grass was allowed to protrude. In the center of the grass plot within the circle was a star-shaped flower bed outlined with bricks, pointed ends up. Inside the star, rising above the tangle of old fashioned roses, altheas and other shrubs, rose several martin houses on poles (literally houses), each with many gables, windows and doors, front porch and even a weather vane on top. The garden adjoined the house on the "up" side and was a delightful place, part vegetables and part flowers. Grass paths with sharply cut edges laid off squares in which the vegetables were planted in neat rows. Beside the paths were the flowers. Originally there may have

Honeysuckle Hill ("Goshen")

been a plan, but after a century it was really a question of survival. Here and there rose giant box bushes and white and purple lilac bushes of incredible size, interspersed with old-fashioned roses, lilacs, phlox, harebells and pinks.

"Now to describe the house. It slipped sideways down the steep hill and was originally on three levels. The kitchen had been raised on stilts to the same level as the dining room, but the parlor was three steps above that level. From the narrow front porch, the steps went up to a small vestibule against the great chimney where hung a peg hatrack. To the right a door opened on the steps down into the dining room. To the left another door led to the parlor. This was a long narrow room with windows on the long sides and a blank wall at the end opposite to the chimney. The shutters were usually kept closed in summer, but the windows had rod holland shades and lace curtains below rather handsome gilt cornice boards. The furniture was set back against the walls, alternating sofas and chairs of various periods, some covered in horsehair, others in brocades. They were interspersed with tables-marble topped, or covered with velvet cloths and holding lamps, books, stereoscopes and ornaments given by relatives at Christmas, or as mementos of travels. Pictures were hung by wire from large porcelain topped nails. I remember the print of "The Doctor" over the high lambrequin-draped mantle, the rather naughty print of the "Peasant in Error", a large framed photgraph of Dr. William Blake, and a group of pictures taken of the reunion of Confederate veterans. This was held at Oakdale by Governor Warfield which Uncle Reuben had attended. There were various family photographs, frequently framed with embroidered mats around them. In the chimney corner to the left of the fireplace, a small staircase wound up to the second floor (giving access to the guest room) which was always spoken of as the "parlor stairs", and to Uncle Som's room. From these two, steps led down into Aunt Pris's room which had two large double beds in it and was usually the quarters for all female guests. I can still see in memory some of the ornaments on the bureau: two glass perfume bottles, one red and one a lovely aqua bohemian glass, treasured because it was given to Aunt Mag and Aunt Pris by Mr. William Corcoran. Then there were some little boxes put together like drawers and tied around with wide satin ribbon with a big bow on top. Each little drawer had attached to its front a hook and eye, button, needle, etc. to indicate the contents supposed to be kept in it. Then there were large cubes of the bigheaded pins needed to fasten veils to hats. A large wardrobe or press seemed to hold everything there was no place for elsewhere. There could not have been left much room for Aunt Pris's clothes. A door led from this room to the landing at the head of the other stairs. This opened onto the "wash room" which gave access to Aunt Emma's room over part of the kitchen. When she married about 1900, this room was furnished with the golden oak of the period and never seemed to be in keeping with the rest of the early Victorian house. Why the "wash room" I do not know. It seemed to be just a passageway with an extra bed for overflow and steps leading up to the attic.

Honeysuckle Hill ("Goshen")

"Returning to the first floor by way of the stairway between the kitchen and dining room walls, we entered the dining room, really the center of the house. The very large fireplace was used for open fires. It had a handsome pair of brass andirons. On the high mantel above was a large Terry clock, a lamp, a box of shotgun shells, and among other ornaments, a china vase kept filled with paper "spills" for lighting lamps, candles, etc. The dining room always seemed small, mainly because the table was large and usually occupied by a large number of people. With the sideboard, and china cupboard, and five doors, the room really was well filled. Wonderful meals were enjoyed there, cooked by Rose and served by Willis, while several of their children, stationed at strategic points, waved "fly-brushes" made of strips of paper nailed to sticks to disperse the flies which rushed in as soon as the shutters were opened. Screens were not considered desirable as they kept out air.

"The kitchen was much larger than the dining room but was the domain of the servants, and I have little recollection of it. Back of the dining room was the shed room, originally a bedroom. Its last occupant was Aunt Rachel Monro, the sister of our great grandmother, and daughter of our Revolutionary ancestor, Dr. Richard Waters. She died there in 1898 at a great age. The old pine cupboard was in the corner of this room. A water cooler on a stand had an unusual feature: a special compartment for butter beneath the water chamber. There was also a bed, washstand, and an old bureau with a cracked glass which should have been properly "restored," but was being kept for Rose because "Sis Pris" had promised it to her. This shed room was used as the passageway to the back yard. Back of the kitchen, the bare earth was swept as clean as a floor. In addition to the usual pump, wood shed, smokehouse and hen house, there was a fattening coop where the last hours of the Plymouth Rocks were spent. A huge iron pot hung from a tripod. In this, the hams were boiled for hours over a fire of smoldering hickory logs.

"Flanked by a huge mulberry tree was the carriage house. In its depths could be glimpsed, behind the currently used carriage and buggies, the "old" carriage with high wheels and sweeping curved springs. This must have dated from the Civil War or before.

"From the corner of the house, along the outside of the white-washed picket fence enclosing the garden, a wide path led to the necessary house (generally designated "Betsy Jones.") On the other side of this path, starting from the carriage house, was a row of outbuildings pertaining to domestic and farm activities: harness house, turkey house, ice house, tool house, various graneries, etc. The path was always kept neatly cut and trimmed of weeds. At the far end was the orchard and finally the family graveyard where the departed Joneses were buried. Here lie Uncle Evan and Aunt Prissie, John and Anne and most of their children including our grandparents; Aquilla and his wife, Rachel and their son Dr. Billy Jones. Before

Honeysuckle Hill ("Goshen")

Aunt Emma's death, the family had the burial plot enclosed in a brick wall and a deed recorded that it was not to be disturbed.

Goshen Servants

"The earliest cook that I remember was Annie whose two small daughters were our playmates. Although their faces were coal black, they bore the names of Lily and Daisy. But most closely associated with Goshen were Willis and Rose Snowden and their numerous progeny. Willis was the son of an old family servant named Suze who left Willis on the Goshen doorstep when she "took up" with a new husband, and went to Washington to live. In my childhood, Crazy Suze was a frequent visitor to the kitchen of our house in Washington. We would be half frightened and half fascinated by her peculiarities of dress and manner. She frequently asked help of my father in having her current "man" arrested for ill-treating her, and then getting him off so he could provide her with firewood and a little food perhaps. Willis was raised at Goshen and gradually became indispensable: coachman, butler, yard man, general factotum. When he married the cook Rose, and started to raise a large family, they provided all the service needed. Willis was highly excitable and very fond of big words, which he misused in a most entertaining way.

"Then there were Tom and Mary Ganitt who lived in their own house down the road. Tom had been one of the field hands and Mary, the daughter of one of their slaves brought by the elder Joneses when they came to Goshen. Mary was very thin and very dark. I remember her as dressed in some of the family best black hand-me-downs, tight fitting basque heavily trimmed with bugles.

"My mother who spent much of her time at "Goshen," talked a great deal of the older servants. Most beloved was Sarah "Aunt Sanny", who loved all the family children and fed them with special delicacies from the kitchen, along with tales and legends of the family past, particularly the O'Neal connection. Lesser lights were old Harriet who was always behindhand and never got around to doing her washing and ironing until Saturday night. Perhaps she was the one whose sewing was done with such oversized stitches that some wag compared her needle and thread to a harrow tooth and well-rope. Or this may have been Amy (or old Ame) who was Suze's mother. The principal story I remember about her was her attempt to cure Uncle Dick of his stammering by hitting him in the face with a raw tongue at butchering time. While his immediate reaction may have been expressed with an unhesitating flow of language, the cure was not permanent.

"Another family by-word was Aaron Brewer. After the war, when newly freed slaves were traveling northward, he appeared at "Goshen" and decided to stay as overseer. He was very powerful and hinted to the other hands that he had been a tribal king in Africa. His name is perpetuated in the family by "Aaron Brewer's stew," a dish he used to concoct for himself from the dry "underneath" part of old ham, browned

Honeysuckle Hill ("Goshen")

in a "dirty skillet" with flour and cream stirred into it.

"The warm and generous hospitality of "Goshen" was enjoyed by many. When the Baltimore Conference met at Goshen Methodist Church, the delegates were always entertained in the home, not only for meals but for overnight. Many friends and relatives were welcome guests at all times. My mother Annie Jones, and her sister Kate, practically lived there during their school days in order to profit by the excellent educational facilities available at the neighborhood school taught by Mr. Paco.

"These recollections of my own are written down for the benefit of the younger generation of Jones descendants who came along too late to enjoy the personal privilege of visiting "Goshen."
Katherine Riggs Poole
November, 1969"

Comments on Katherine Riggs Poole's Memories

When she visited "Goshen" before her death, she told the present owner Dr. McFarland that the children were never allowed to go into the attic.

Doctor William Jones, son of Evan Jones and Mary O'Neale, and brother to John Jones, was born on April 12, 1790 near Rockville, Montgomery County, Maryland. His father was a respected farmer of Welsh descent, but William chose a different vocation due to the persuasion of Rev. John Breckinridge, a Presbyterian minister and friend. He was given a classical education at Rockville Academy and then placed as a student of medicine under Dr. William Tyler of Frederick, Maryland. Afterwards, he was sent to attend course lectures at the University of Pennsylvania, from which he graduated. He was an army surgeon in the War of 1812 where he remained until 1815 and then went into private practice with Dr. James Blake of Washington DC. On December 21, 1821, He married Miss Sarah L. Corcoran, daughter of Thomas Corcoran Sr. of Georgetown, with whom he lived happily until her death September 24, 1843.

Doctor Jones became interested in politics early in life and was elected a number of times to the Washington City Council. He was a member of the celebrated Central Committee in Washington and became an ardent Jackson supporter. When General Jackson became president in 1829, he appointed Dr. Jones Postmaster of the city, a post he held through Jackson's terms and part of Van Buren's term. He was again appointed under Tyler's administration on July 10, 1841 to 1845 and then again during Buchanan's administration from 1858 to 1861. His entire service in this office was nearly 17 years.

Honeysuckle Hill ("Goshen")

Doctor Jones, a fair and impartial man, was of unimpeachable integrity. Although he was a strong partisan, he was highly respected by everyone, particularly Jackson and Tyler. He never entirely relinquished his profession, practicing through a period of fifty years. He was never known to make a charge for his service where he knew circumstances would make payment difficult. He was a member of the Washington Monument Society and president of the Medical Society of the District of Columbia. He was a professing Christian and a member of the Episcopal Church. His death occurred on June 25, 1867 in his 78th year.

The William J. Jones, M.D. who is buried in the Jones Family Cemetery, was the son of Evan A. and Rachel Jones. Evan was Emma's brother. He is the William Jones who "died young," as stated in Katherine Poole's memories. He graduated from the University of Maryland in 1883 and specialized in throat care. He settled in Baltimore and for many years was associated with Bay View Asylum as a resident doctor. He died at 37 of Bright's Disease.

Courtesy of Joyce Hawkins   *Honeysuckle Hill (Goshen)*

Honeysuckle Hill ("Goshen")

History of the City Post Office by Madison Davis Vol. VI (p. 123) MCHS,

Katherine Poole's Memories, MCHS,

Gladys King, Goshen History, Goshen Homemakers Club

Self

Courtesy of The Montgomery County Historical Society

JOHN SPRIGG POOLE

Annie Evelyn Jones Poole

MARTHA SPRIGG POOLE

KATHERINE RIGGS POOLE

Honeysuckle Hill ("Goshen")

GENEALOGY OF KATHERINE RIGGS POOLE

1. Evan Jones m. Mary O'Neale
2.   son - John Jones m. Anne Smith Waters
3.   son - Evan Acquilla Jones m. Rachel Riggs
4.   dau. - Annie Evelyn Jones m. John Sprigg Poole
5.   dau. - Martha Sprigg Poole, and Katherine Riggs Poole

Dorothy Peugh MCHS

Self

Jones Family Cemetery

JONES FAMILY CEMETERY

The Jones family cemetery is located adjacent to the family home, Honeysuckle Hill ("Goshen"). Here lies buried about 14 members and descendants of the John Jones family. The oldest tombstone is that of John Jones, 1788-1847. Before Emma Jones died in 1924, the family built a brick wall, about five feet high, to surround the graveyard with no steps leading in, but with six steps leading out. The cemetery was landscaped with boxwood trees that now stand about eight feet high and are overgrown and twisted with honeysuckle, as is the entire cemetery. The following people, with their epitaphs and dates as listed on their stones, are buried here:

John Jones: died June 26, 1847, aged 59, "Blessed in the Lord."

Ann S. Jones: wife of John Jones, died March 25, 1859, aged 62, "Blessed are the pure in heart for they shall see God."

Richard W. Jones: born Sept. 1828, died May 4, 1895, "He will be our guide even unto death" Psalms VIII v.14

Margaret A. Jones: died Dec. 24, 1877, aged 54, "As for me, I will behold thy face in rightness, I shall be satisfied when I awake in thy likeness."

Evan A Jones: In memory of Evan A. Jones, born Sept. 9, 1826, died March 22, 1904 aged 77 years, 6 months and 13 days.

Rachel G. Jones: In memory of Rachel G. wife of Evan A. Jones, born July 9, 1836, died June 21, 1896, "My time are in thy hands, My God I wish them there, My life, my friends, my soul I leave entirely to thy care."

William J. Jones: died March 26, 1853, aged 20, "Not lost, but gone before."

Somerset Orme Jones: Nov. 8, 1835 - Apr. 22, 1914

Priscilla J. Jones: Nov 6, 1825 - Feb. 18, 1908, "There is no rest for the weary"

Eugene W. Jones: died Nov. 19, 1872, aged 34, "In Jesus I put my trust."

Jones Family Cemetery

Emma Jones: wife of Reuben Riggs, April 24, 1840 - April 26, 1929, "The Lord is my Shepherd, I shall not want."

Nannie: Daughter of Wm T. & E.R. Jones, born April 5, 1869, died July 22, 1877, "Loved in life, In death remembered"
(E. R. Jones is Elizabeth who married her first cousin William T. Jones, and their daughter was Nannie.)

William J. Jones MD: In memory of W.J. Jones, MD, born Dec. 4, 1856, died Jan. 10, 1894, aged 37.
(He was called Dr. Billy Jones and was the son of Evan A. & Rachel Jones.)

Annie P. Linthicum: died Nov. 24, 1869, aged 26, "Though he slay me, yet, will I trust in him."
(Annie was the granddaughter of John and Ann Jones. Her parents were Mary Ellen Jones Linthicum and Lloyd Linthicum.)

Photo by Richard F. Boggs — Interior of Jones Family Cemetery

Photo by Richard F. Boggs — Exterior of Jones Family Cemetery

Jones Family Cemetery

Nancy Schively - historical notes

Self

FERTILE MEADOWS
Mill Owner's Dwelling

This home was purchased in 1933 by Lee and Brita Councilman. During their ownership it was beautifully restored, with a wing added in the back where Brita displayed her glass collection on glass shelves attached to the windows. Beautiful antiques collected by the Councilmans furnished the interior. The former mill sites had been cleaned out and the natural overgrowth began to fill in the empty spaces. The once raging creek became a quiet stream, providing water for the grazing cows from the nearby dairy farm, Green Hills. In 1987 Green Hills Farm was sold for development.

Part of this home was probably built before 1800 by Joshua Pigman. By 1790, there were recorded two mills, a copper mine, mill dams and races, and a log cabin used for a mill store on property referred to as Pigmans Purchase. By 1797, Edward Crowe owned land grants referred to as Land of Goshen, Benjamin Square, Pigmans Purchase, and Fertile Meadows. He purchased four plots or 150 acres from Reverend Ignatius Pigman for 125 pounds sterling. After making improvements on the dwelling and property, Crowe sold it to Sam Robertson and his wife Rachel in 1803. They were from Annapolis and were eager to make their fortune in the mill business. Both Sam and Rachel are buried behind the dwelling with some of their children. About 1817, George Washington Riggs purchased the property at public auction from trustees representing the Robertson Estate, for $13,115.00. Although G.W. Riggs never lived there, he hired millers to operate the mills. He was a well-to-do man, having made his fortune in the import and export business, and as a silversmith. His grand home called "Woodville" was located outside of Baltimore, Maryland. In his earlier years, he owned property in Georgetown, where he lived and operated his businesses. Remus D. Riggs inherited the Goshen Mills in 1859, which stayed in the family until 1916.

When the Councilmans purchased Fertile Meadows, they also bought the Goshen Post Office and Store property at public sale. They paid a mere $800.00. Lee Councilman died in 1965 and Brita died in 1980. Since her passing, the property deteriorated due to subsequent owner mismanagement and financial problems. The land, with the residence, was sold to a developer who is presently building single family homes there. The developer is also obligated by the county to restore the original home (mill owner's residence) as it is listed as an historical home.

Fertile Meadows

Brita Day Councilman and her husband Lee, who was a well known attorney in the Washington area, are buried behind their home next to the Robertsons who owned the property in the early 1800's.

Courtesy of The Sentinel Montgomery County

Brita Dyberg Counselman, circa 1910.

Laytonsville resident grande dame is dead

Brita Dyberg Counselman, a socialite and resident of two continents who lived most of her life in Montgomery County, died Sunday of pneumonia. She was 89.

Born in 1890 in Oakland, Calif., of immigrant Swedish parents, Counselman lived the past 47 years near Laytonsville on a hundred-acre estate known as Fertile Meadows, whose 18th century home she meticulously restored.

She founded and organized the Republican Women's Club of Upper Montgomery County, and was an active promoter of social legislation concerning children and mental health.

A beautiful woman, Counselman, while living in New York in the early 1910's pursuing an acting career, sat for sketches that appeared in the Saturday Evening Post and other magazines. One account reports that she stopped traffic in New York when a policeman saw her, blew his whistle and exclaimed: "I was dreaming of a rose in the Devil's garden, turned around, and there you were!"

A 1910 graduate of Mills College, she became the first woman to sell insurance for New York Life.

She and her husband, Freeman Day, moved to Washington in 1913, when he was appointed assistant attorney general by President Woodrow Wilson. While living here, she became friends with Supreme Court Associate Justice Oliver Wendell Holmes and a member of his Friday Afternoon Discussion Group.

She later returned to New York, and also lived in Paris between 1920 and 1930, during which time she divorced Day and married Montgomery County native Lee Counselman, who had been general manager of National Cash Register and co-founder of Chalmers Motor Company. The two returned here, and in 1933 bought Fertile Meadows, part of the Gaither family land grant. The house had been used as a post office, call Goshen, in 1879.

Lee Counselman died in 1965. She is survived by two sons, Dr. Robert Day of Middleburg, Va., and John A. Day of Layfayette Hill, Pa., nine grandchildren and three great-grandchildren. The family requests expressions of sympathy be made in the form of contributions to the Humane Society of the United States, 2100 L St., NW, Washington, D.C.

Photo by Ardith G. Boggs

Courtesy of Joyce Hawkins *Fertile Meadows*

Fertile Meadows

Riggs family oral histories.

Gladys King History, Goshen Homemakers Club

History of Goshen Mills and Immediate Area, Goshen Mills Chapter, National Society Daughters of the American Revolution

History of Early Water Mills in Montgomery County, Eleanor Cook MCHS

Self

SYCAMORE HOLLOW on WILDCAT CREEK

In 1650, Robert Brooke came to St. Mary's County. He sailed from England in his own ship to settle a royal land grant titled "Della Brooke", bringing with him his family and servants. This land grant was of enormous proportions. Three generations later, James Brooke came to what is now Montgomery County in 1723. His son received a land grant of 15,000 acres which extended from Sandy Spring to Germantown. This portion, including what we know today as "Sycamore Hollow," was later sold by Gerard Brooke to a Dorsey, perhaps Patuxent John, his son (Sam?), or Grandson Henry (sometimes referred to as Harry) Woodward Dorsey of Anne Arundel County, about 1814-1816. Earlier in 1798, Henry (Harry) Woodward Dorsey of Anne Arundel County purchased 385 and 1/2 acres of Resurvey on Benjamin Square and Lodowicks Range from Richard Ridgely. The Dorsey line is Henry (Harry) Woodward Dorsey who also inherited "Dorsey's Search," "Sam's Lot," and "Pleasant Valley," from his father (or Grandfather) known as "Patuxent John", Captain of Militia in 1742 in Maryland. Patuxent John was married to Eleanor Woodward. Prior to him there was an Edward Dorsey, then Capt. John Dorsey of Baltimore County, who was a Justice for Anne Arundel County, 1694-1697. Edward Dorsey who settled in Anne Arundel County probably came from "Hockley in the Hole" in Warwickshire, England about 1650 or earlier. Parts of these land grants have stood in St. Mary's, Prince Georges, Frederick, and finally Montgomery County.

Henry Woodward Dorsey's first wife was Mary Macubbin whom he married on February 21, 1786. She was the daughter of Zachariah Macubbin. After her death, Henry married Rachel Magruder Cooke. Henry and Rachel had a son named Harry Woodward Dorsey who married Sarah Ann Waters in 1829. She was the daughter of Ignatius and Elizabeth Dorsey Waters. When she died, he married her sister Susan Maria Waters in 1844. Susan's half sister-in-law Harriet Woodward Dorsey, married Sam Blunt in 1818. In 1852 Susan and Harriet worked together on a quilt which is called the "Woodbourne" quilt. This quilt has been displayed at various museums, including the DAR Constitution Hall in Washington D.C. "Woodbourne" is the name of the historical home built by Sam Blunt.

Prior to James Brooke's arrival in 1723, there were a few squatter's and hunter's cabins scattered in the area. On the property which was to become "Sycamore Hollow" sat a log cabin with a balcony. A huge fireplace, large enough to burn logs up to five feet long, dominated the lower level. In 1720, an addition was built on to the small cabin which included the area of the modern kitchen, a second floor bed chamber, and a third floor bed chamber. In 1740 another addition was built which included an area for a dining room,

Sycamore Hollow on Wildcat Creek

a bed chamber, and slave quarters for the house slaves. The slave cubicles were removed in 1953. About 1800, the next addition was built that was the largest and tallest portion of the house. The hall opens to all three floors; the great room, two second floor bed chambers, and a third floor bed chamber. Lightning was said to have struck this section, which burned, and was rebuilt around 1840. "The stairs in this section are unsupported and boast walnut handrails and chestnut ballisters. Dolphin scrolls grace the side of each riser. Fine moldings, a curved window, and a curved door lend individuality."* On the curve of the stairs, between the first and second floors, were two curved niches painted with scenes of the French Alps by a primitive painter named LeBlanc. It was said that he was homesick for his beloved mountains and painted the identical scenes in other homes as far away as Brunswick, Maryland.

After the lightning fire occurred, only one candelabrum remained. This was made up of seventy two parts and was hand threaded. Each part had to be numbered when removed for cleaning. The paneling in the great room was of Honduras Mahogany and the floors of walnut, one and one half inches thick. Medallions in the ceiling lent elegance to both the great room and the lower hall.

Before Mr. and Mrs. Charles Burton purchased this property in the 1950's, Mrs. Burton said it was referred to as "Long Meadows" and was owned by a man named Hinkly.

"In 1960, the lines of the early, one room deep, Maryland telescope house were altered as unobtrusively as possible. A rear wing was added to give utility to the twentieth century way of life."* This wing included a glassed porch, powder room, laundry, work room, storage area, and garage. A staircase that had originally been part of "Thomas Delight," a 1670 Thomas Dashiell property on Maryland's Eastern Shore, was removed and numbered piece by piece. It was transported to "Sycamore Hollow", reassembled and put in place as the staircase leading to the balcony in the original part of the house, the hunter's cabin. It was hand carved by an indentured craftsman.

Lightning again took its toll in 1968 when the entire third floor of the tallest addition was devastated by fire, smoke, and water.

In the early 1980's a large addition was added as a wing to the back of the house. It is one great room with a fireplace and open ceiling, two stories high with a large skylight.

It was a sad day for the Goshen community and present owners the Burtons, when the home fell victim once again to fire. This time it was in 1988 and caused by faulty wiring in a kitchen range overhead fan. The distruction was devastating, heavily damaging much of this home, including the fine antiques lovingly collected over the years. Mrs. Burton is a world renowned rug hooker and designer. Many of her priceless rugs were also badly damaged or destroyed. Through sheer

Sycamore Hollow on Wildcat Creek

determination and large support given the Burtons by neighbors, family, and friends, they were able to restore their home, and remaining antiques. To do this they moved a large mobile home onto the property so they could oversee the restoration. The paintings in the curved niches on the staircase were restored by a local painter, Joan Leydon. Two years later, the Burtons were once again entertaining friends and family at Sycamore Hollow. The house is 105 feet long and has seventeen different levels, including the two attics and basement.

This home today is magnificent, and stands as a proud reminder of the rich history of Goshen and its people.

Photo by Richard F. Boggs   Sycamore Hollow

circ. 1973

Sycamore Hollow on Wildcat Creek

Waters Family History, MCHS

* Sycamore Hollow on Wildcat Creek, Montgomery County Maryland, Mary Burton

History of Early Water Mills in Montgomery County Md., Eleanor Cook MCHS

Mary Burton oral history

Self

ATWOOD-BLUNT HOME

Sadly, this home has been burned down because it was declared unsafe. It was a very early home, around 1700, with the original kitchen in the basement. It was located on Huntmaster Road, not far from Avalon.

Courtesy of Joyce Hawkins *Atwood-Blunt Home*

Avalon

AVALON

Avalon is located at 9401 Huntmaster Road (formerly Blunt). This home is the site of an earlier Harry Woodward Dorsey Blunt home that was destroyed by fire in 1918. Both Harry Woodward Dorsey Blunt and his son, Harry Woodward Blunt Jr., were owners of Avalon. The present home was built sometime later on the original foundation.

The Blunts have been traced from the eastern shore; but because of the mysterious disappearance of old church records from the Episcopal Church on Kent Island, there remain some unanswered questions. An old piece of paper found at Avalon stated the following information: Samuel Blunt married Miss Mary Ringgold. Their children Joseph, Araminta, and Sallie never married. An unnamed daughter married a Mr. Holk, and their son Samuel married Miss Dorsey. A 1790 census lists Samuel Blunt as having a household consisting of one male over 16, one male under 16, five females and 11 slaves.

When son Samuel moved to Washington, DC and then on to Montgomery County, he married Harriet Woodward Dorsey in 1818. She was the daughter of Harry Woodward Dorsey and Mary Macubbin of Sycamore Hollow in Goshen. After they married, they lived at the Woodbourne Estate. An old letter found there clearly connects the Blunts with the Eastern Shore. The letter dated 1859 was written by Harry Woodward Dorsey Blunt (of Avalon). In it he is asking his brother Atwood to urge their father Samuel to write to the Eastern Shore concerning their Aunt Sally's legacy.

Harry Woodward Blunt Jr. cut quite a dapper figure with his straw hat. He was a gentleman farmer who, according to some, had a popular sideline: moonshine.

Earlier this year (1993) the great-great-great-grandson of Samuel and Harriet Blunt, William Barton Hungerford Jr., moved to Goshen Valley Court on the former Green Hills Farm property just a short distance from his great-great-grandfather's home, Avalon. He lives there with his wife Mary, and triplets Benedetto John, William Barton, and Mary Christine.

Avalon has been the site of many fox hunts over the years.

Courtesy of Joyce Hawkins

Avalon

Avalon

Harrison King, oral history

Gladys King History, Goshen Homemakers Club

Sam Riggs, oral history

Dixie Hungerford, oral history

1776 Our Ancestors; Patriot or Tory, by Edith Lloyd Blunt

Self

BLACK and WHITE INN

This house, located at the intersection of Goshen and Warfield Roads, is said to be about 120 years old, having been built about 1870. It was originally one of the local blacksmith shops, and was in use until 1920. At that time the blacksmith, who was a black man, was named Claggett. In the 1970's, there was an old house standing on the very back of this property that housed a family named Claggett. Many of the outbuildings that were the site of the original shop have been torn down. The garage-like structure that stands on Warfield Road may have been used as the shop in the early part of this century. However, back in the days when it was a beehive of activity, this was a large two story barn, where square dances were held on the second floor.

Back in 1879, the blacksmith listed in the Goshen Directory was C. F. Hogan. Since the Black and White Inn dates back to the 1870's, it is likely that Hogan was located there. The 1880 Goshen Directory listed a James Campbell as blacksmith. Two blacksmiths, Barber and Scheckles, were listed in the 1882 Goshen Directory. It isn't totally clear where the earlier blacksmith shops were located. One blacksmith site, shown on an early map, was on Goshen Road between the Goshen Store and The Goshen Mills Complex.

The Black and White Inn is said to have operated as an Inn in the late 1800's and early 1900's. The black gentry from Washington would come out to the country for weekend outings to picnic, and to discuss news and politics. As late as the 1980's, there stood a row of motel-like cabins along the Warfield Road side of this property, reminiscent of the days when it was operated as an Inn.

Mr. Charles Harris, who was also a black man, lived there many years until his death about 1990. He operated a candy store in the basement of his house for the children of the area. In the 1970's and early 1980's, children, with their bicycles, were frequently found congregating around his back door drinking soda pop and sharing candy bars. At Christmas, many children would drop off Christmas cookies and gifts to this kindly gentleman and his wife. The site is now owned by the private school next door.

Courtesy of Joyce Hawkins   Black and White Inn

Black and White Inn

Gladys King History, Goshen Homemakers Club

Charles Harris, oral history

History of Goshen Mills and Immediate Area by The Goshen Mills Chapter, National Society DAR

Self

John Samuel Davis Homestead and Mill

JOHN SAMUEL DAVIS HOMESTEAD AND MILL

John Samuel Davis, son of Joshua Benjamin Davis and Margaret Ann Poole, was born December 1, 1838. He had at least three brothers and sisters. His grandfather was also John Davis (1810 - 1847); he is buried in the Dunkard Graveyard at Monrovia, Maryland.

John Samuel Davis was a serious, hard-working man who was very proud of his Welsh ancestry. He was employed as a miller for the Goshen Mills (Riggs Mills) from 1860-69. He left to operate his own mill, purchased from Washington D. Waters. His mill was located on Wildcat Creek, near what is now known as Davis Mill Road. His home was situated on Blunt Road, on top of a hill overlooking the mill. Here he and his wife, Mary Ellen Phoebus, raised their family. Fourteen children were born. Eleven survived to adulthood. Two sons, William and John, died in infancy, along with a daughter, Lillian. Sadly his wish for a son was never realized. He was very strict with his eleven daughters.

Although he did not enlist during the Civil War, John Davis spoke of how he and his family ground flour and baked bread all night long for the troops who were passing through.

John Samuel, Mary Ellen, and an unmarried daughter, Martha, are buried in the graveyard at "Old Goshen Church." This church is located on Brink Road (formerly Goshen Road). The church was leased to the Mennonites in the 1950's. Very little remains of his home and mill, but the enclosed photos show how it looked during their occupancy, and again in the mid 1970's.

A complete history of John Samuel Davis, his family and descendants follows, which was written by family members. Elmira Davis Harper Dietrich compiled the history, drew the sketches of the mill and house owned by John Samuel Davis, as well as the map of its location. The location of the Goshen Methodist Church is incorrect on the map.

The history of his mills and property, previous owners, and land grants, can be found in Chapter I, titled "Goshen: From the Beginning."

John Samuel Davis

Courtesy of John Edward Burdette

Courtesy of John Edward Burdette   *John Samuel Davis Homestead*

Courtesy of John Edward Burdette *Davis Mill*

John Samuel Davis Homestead and Mill

Davis Family History; Elmira Davis Harper Detrich

John Edward Burdette of Damascus, Md.

Gladys King History, Goshen Homemakers Club

History of Early Water Mills In Montgomery County, Md. by Eleanor M. V. Cook, MCHS

Self.

THE DAVIS FAMILY AND ITS COAT OF ARMS

Motto: Authorities consulted show no motto for these arms. However, "Ne tentes, aut perfice" (Do not attempt, or else accomplish) is listed in Fairbain's "Book of Crests of the Families of Great Britain and Ireland", as associated with the Davis family.

Arms: Gules a chevron ermine in chief two mounds or in base a talbot passant of the last.

Crest: Two arms embowed habited ermine cuffs azure hands proper supporting a mound, as in the arms.

The exhaustive work, "The Davis Family" by H. A. Davis published in 1927 will prove extremely interesting to those seeking information concerning this family from its legendary origin to modern times. Apparently, this family can be traced back several centuries B.C., and includes Constantine the Great as one of its members.

The adoption of surnames began in England soon after the subjugation of the Saxons by the Normans, under William the Conqueror in 1066. Many old records reveal the Davis family as well established in Wales about that time, and it is presumed that Davis, Daviss, David, et cetera, are all various spellings of the same family name. Jefferson Davis, the president of the Confederate States appears to be descended from Morgan Davis, who settled in the Province of Pennsylvania prior to 1686.

One of the earliest members of the Davis family to come to America was Thomas Davis, who came on the "Margaret" to James City, Va. in 1619. He is believed to have been the grandson of Sir Thomas Davis of the London Company, and to have occupied a position of importance in the social and political affairs of the colony. He married Elizabeth Pierpont.

Before the end of the 17th century, branches of the Davis family were to be found in the many communities surrounding the Chesapeake Bay, as well as in Delaware and Pennsylvania.

Today members of the old distinguished family are to be found in every state in the Union, and they are well represented in the arts, sciences and professions, as well as in the world of commerce. Some of the contributions which members of this family have made to the cultural and economic development of the New World are recorded in the following references:

1. Ancestral Records and Portraits, Vol. I published by Grafton Press

2. Compendium of American Genealogy, Vol. 4 - Virkus, published by Morris Bros. de Villers and Co., Inc., 254 W. 34th Street, New York, New York 10001.

John Davis

Joshua Benjamin Davis
married

Margaret Ann Poole

B 1-1-1810
D 7-16-1847

B 8-25-1813
D

7 Children

Robert Davis

Sarah Ann Davis

George Allen Davis

Margaret Ann Davis

Hamilton Davis

Elizabeth Davis

*John Samuel Davis

*John Samuel Davis   Born 12- 1-1838

                           Died 8- 7-1922

        Married   3-15-1860

   Mary Ellen Phoebus   B   3-12-1842

                            D   7-19-1913

Of this union __14__ children were born

    I. Martha Virginia   1861-1925
   II. Margaret Ann   1862-1901
  III. Katie Dorsey   1864-1946
   IV. John Jefferson   1866-1867
    V. Marietta   1868-1960
   VI. Alverta   1870-1939
  VII. Emma Augusta   1871-1933
 VIII. Lillian   1873-1873
   IX. Laura May   1874-1963
    X. Johanna   1876-1942
   XI. Bessie Ellen   1879-1957
  XII. Eva Maude   1882-1969
 XIII. Adeline Gartside   1887-1968
  XIV. William Albert   1888-1888

The branch of the Davis family in which we are most interested goes back to John Davis who is buried in the Dunkard Graveyard at Monrovia, Maryland. His son, Joshua Benjamin Davis (1810-1847) married Margaret Ann Poole. To them were born at least seven children, the youngest of whom was John Samuel Davis.

Upon the death of his parents, John Samuel went to live with his uncle, Washington Poole at Monrovia, Md. Here he worked in his uncle's mill learning the trade which he was to follow all his life. Here he also met Mary Ellen Phoebus from New Market, Md., whom he married in 1860. He ran several mills, but for many years before his death, he ran the grist and saw mill near Goshen which burned shortly after his death.

He was a sober, hard working man, and was very strict with his eleven girls. Probably his greatest wish was for a son but both sons born to him died in infancy. He often talked about his Welsh ancestry. Although he did not enlist during the Civil War, he told of grinding flour all night for the men who were passing through, and of his family baking bread all night for them.

Martha Virginia Davis was born February 25, 1861, the first daughter of John and Mary Ellen Davis. She attended Goshen School and Goshen Methodist Church and had the normal happy life of a girl of her period. She was active in the Church and sang in the choir.

As a girl in her teens it seemed that Mattie developed a talent for homemaking which was to continue until the family home was closed at the passing of her father. She became an excellent cook and relieved her mother of much of the preparation of the meals. As the family grew she was a second mother to the little sisters.

In that era there were few professions open to women and not many girls ventured away from the family home until they were married. Mattie never married, but she seemed content to stay at home with her parents until the death of her mother. Then she continued to make a home for her father and "kept the home fires burning" for the married sisters and their families whenever they returned to visit the old homestead. She loved all the members of the family and was always so happy to see any of them. She never was too tired or too ill to provide a big meal for one guest or a dozen.

Aunt Mattie never had a career as such, never belonged to a club, took little part in the social life of the neighborhood but to those of us who can remember her, she will be remembered for her loving care for all who were under her roof. This loving care was evidenced in such homey ways as her concern over any member of the family being out in the cold and wet. She always welcomed them home with dry garments and a warm drink.

The following are some recollections of the nieces and nephews.

"The thing we remember most is how quickly Aunt Mattie could add to the supply of food she was preparing for Sunday dinner. Perhaps there would already be several members of the family there and she would see another car coming down the road. She would very swiftly kill another chicken, dress it and add it to those ready for the pan."

"I remember, when I was a tiny little girl, Aunt Mattie would come out to the car, when we arrived, take my face between her hands and kiss me. I remember her infinite patience with a little girl who wanted to be at her heels while she baked biscuits. She even provided the child with a small pan and a piece of dough. I also love to remember the quiet afternoons that were sometimes lonely for a little girl raised in the city. So often Aunt Mattie cut a plate of her famous Cold Water Cake (has anyone in the family the recipe?) and put the cake on the dining room table where I could help myself. If she thought I was especially lonely, she'd add lemonade to the treat."

A nephew remembers the rather unusual way she had of cutting the big fresh loaves of homemade bread and her way of calling us to the table with "get in your stalls".

Mattie lived for a time with several of her sisters after the old home was closed. Wherever she was she kept busy -- helping in the kitchen and trying to make everyone in that particular household comfortable.

She passed away October 15, 1925 in Washington where she had been living with her youngest sister. She was laid to rest in the family plot in Goshen Cemetery, but she continues to live in the hearts of those of us who were privileged to know her.

The second daughter, Margaret Ann, married William Bennett. They moved to Hagerstown, Md. and here their two sons were born. Margaret Ann, known to her family as "Mag", died at the age of 39. She, too, is buried at Goshen. After her death, William Bennett and his two sons, John and Roger, moved in with John Samuel Davis and his wife. Mr. Bennett and his son John soon moved on to the mill at Clappers, Md., but Roger remained at the mill with his grandfather Davis until he was grown.

The third daughter, Katie Dorsey, married Oscar Kurts Poale from Barnesville, Md., where they lived and kept the General Merchandise store. After her husband's death, Katie, her daughter Mabel and her son-in-law moved to Gaithersburg, Md. Here she lived until her death in 1946. She is buried with her husband in the Monocacy Cemetery at Beallsville, Md.

The fourth child, John Jefferson, lived less than a year.

The fifth child, Marietta, (called Mollie) early became a needlewoman and used that talent until her old age. She met her husband, Luther Edwin Harper, from Baltimore, while he was visiting his aunt, Mrs. Benson, who was a neighbor of the Davis family. After their marriage at the Davis home they went to Baltimore. Mr. Harper, whose mother, Elmira, had died when he was very young, boarded with friends. Here he took his bride, but they soon started housekeeping. Since his salary as a clerk for the Poole Engineering Company in Woodbury was small, "Mollie" had a Lutheran and a Presbyterian Minister as roomers. After their home was paid for, she devoted much of her spare time to her sewing, embroidery and knitting. After they moved to their home on Roland Avenue, they joined the Otterbein United Brethren Church which was nearby. Both became active in the church, Marietta in the "Ladies Aid," while her husband was Superintendant of the Sunday School for many years, also "General Steward". Their daughter often told of going to church five times every Sunday. Marietta was a "homebody" and lived in that same house until she died at 92. Both she and her husband "Ed" are buried in the Mausoleum of the Lorraine Cemetery in Baltimore.

Alverta, the sixth child married Ignatius Ward from Woodfield, Md. They raised seven children and spent most of their married life in Gaithersburg where Mr. Ward was a builder and contractor. They are buried at Forest Oak Cemetery in Gaithersburg, Md.

Emma Augusta, the seventh child, married James Purdum from Cedar Grove, Md. Both Purdum boys were known as exceptionally fine farmers, so "Gus" and "Jim" Purdum soon moved to a large farm in Cedar Grove and they too raised seven children. They are buried in the Cedar Grove Baptist Church Cemetery.

The eighth child, Lillian, lived less than a year.

Laura May, the ninth child, also married a Cedar Grove man, Joseph Purdum, a brother of James Purdum. She also moved to Cedar Grove where a boy and a girl were born to her. The daughter, Marietta died in infancy and her son, Rufus, lived to be only twenty five years old. Her husband, Joe, lived to be only 38. Joe and Laura bought the Riggs farm and lived there until Joe's death. Then she moved to Baltimore for a short time, then to Gaithersburg, where her son died. After her son's death, she married Benjamin Hughes and moved to Washington, D. C. She spent her last years in the Baptist Home in Washington. Her son, grandson and husband, Joe are buried with her in the Cedar Grove Baptist Church Cemetery. Mr. Hughes is buried in Rockville.

Johanna, the tenth child, married Robert Hays Bowman from Cedar Grove. After their marriage they lived on the Bowman family farm where their first three children were born. Later they moved to a farm in Cedar Heights. Here their three youngest children were born. In 1924, they moved to Washington, D. C. where both Johanna and her husband died. They are buried in the Cedar Grove Methodist Church Cemetery.

The eleventh child, Bessie Ellen, attended Montgomery County schools and was very active in the Goshen Methodist Church during her earlier years. She sang in the church choir where she was given voice lessons. In April of 1899, Bessie Ellen was married, to Hezekiah Barber of Cedar Grove, in the Goshen Methodist Church. For a short time after their marriage they made their home in Cedar Grove so Bessie moved her membership to the Salem Methodist Church. From Cedar Grove they moved to a small farm near Woodfield where they raised tobacco as the chief crop. Later they moved to a dairy farm near Clarksburg. In 1924 the family moved to Washington, D.C. where Mr. Barber held several positions as a security guard until his retirement. Bessie Ellen found time to continue her sewing, visiting the sick as well as keeping her home. Both Bessie and Hezekiah are buried in the Salem Methodist Church Cemetery.

Eva Maude Davis was born on December 1, 1882, and judging from stories she tells, had a most happy childhood. She attended Goshen School and was active in Goshen Methodist Church and Sunday School. She has often spoken of preparing, under the direction of Prof. Waters, for the Children's Day Services. These services were popular, not only with the members of Goshen Church, but other folks in the community as well.

Olin Austin Walter was born at Boyds, Maryland on February 9, 1886 to Robert Bruce and Sarah Deborah Walter. When still a small boy he moved with his family to Kensington, Maryland. He attended the local school, and in his spare time was constantly at his father's heels as he went about his work of carpentering. Later he and his father worked in the woodworking shop at the Department of Agriculture. Both Olin and his father were cabinet makers, but his father in later years said that Olin's work far exceeded his own as Olin's work had a certain finish that gave the completed product a professional appearance.

Eva and Olin met when Eva accompanied her cousin on a trip to the Walter home to visit one of the daughters of the family. It was almost love at first sight with both of them and they were engaged some time later. After a courtship of two years they were married on August 17, 1909. Because of her mother's ill health the wedding took place at the home of Robert and Johanna Bowman at Cedar Grove. After the wedding supper the bridal couple boarded the train at Germantown for the trip to Washington where they were to make their home during all of their married life. Their first home was a house in the Northwest section of Washington which they shared with another young couple. They later moved to an apartment near Washington Circle where Helen Louise was born on January 19, 1911. Some months later they moved into the Northeast area, to an apartment in the home of the Taylor family. When Helen was about three years old the family bought the house at 921 K Street, N. E. and that was home for over forty years.

This was just an average couple--trying to be good citizens and training their only child in that way. They worked very hard to build a solid home and their home was always open to friends and relatives. Eva's greatest joy was to be able to help a relative or anyone experiencing illness or any sort of trouble. The hour was never too late, or she was never too tired, to go to one in need.

Olin joined the Masons in the early years and, while he loved Masonry as long as he lived, he never took an active part because he was too much of a home body. However, he did enjoy the meetings, was proud of being a Mason, and was always ready to help when called upon.

During the early years he transferred from the Department of Agriculture to the Bureau of Standards where he worked, first as a cabinet maker and later as a pattern maker, until his forced retirement from the Government Service in the early 1930's due to President Roosevelt's economy measure which retired all employees with thirty years service.

During the years just before and while Helen was in high school Eva worked on the contingent force at Lansburgh's. She was so successful in her work that she worked almost continuously rather than only part time. Her cheerfulness and eagerness to serve endeared her to her customers and the Department Managers were eager to have her work for them.

Eva never worked after 1932 and, when Olin was retired, they had a good life together, enjoying their home and taking brief trips in the summer, until Olin's passing on February 24, 1950.

Adaline Gartside, born March 3, 1887, was the youngest daughter of John and Mary Ellen Davis. Because of her being the "baby" she was somewhat spoiled and the pet of her parents as well as the older sisters who were like second mothers to her. The love her family and relatives held for her is evidenced in two little stories she told the writer just weeks before her passing. When she was very small she had wanted a pair of red shoes and one of her older sisters had walked all over Hagerstown, going into every store, trying to find those red shoes for Baby Sister. The other incident she mentioned was the devotion she and Uncle Allen Davis had for each other. She said at the time she was leaving home to buy her trousseau, Uncle Allen was sitting in the swing which was beneath her bedroom window. She couldn't bear to tell him goodbye so she wrapped a note around her picture and tossed it out of the window to him. She added that his children told her, after his passing, that he was clutching her picture in his hand when he died.

Addie had a great capacity for fun and was a very lively person. This quality continued throughout her life. She was also a most generous person, sharing her substance with anyone who was ill or in need, and she was equally anxious to share even when there was no need, just for the joy of giving. This was particularly true with her children and grandchildren. She and Eva, being the two youngest girls, were very close as they grew up and Addie so many times laughingly told about how she would tickle Eva to get her own way when persuasion failed. She always spoke of a very happy childhood while attending Goshen School and taking an active part in Goshen Methodist Church.

On December 20, 1906 she married Reginald Darby Poole, the son of Lucretia and Kurts Poole of Buck Lodge, Maryland. Darby bought a farm near his family home and had it waiting for his bride when they were married. Two sons were born there, Reginald Leroy on October 6, 1907 and Olin Darby on October 15, 1910. After her marriage Addie joined the Methodist Church at Poolesville which was her church home as long as the family lived in Maryland. Some years later they had the misfortune to have their home and all their belongings burned. They lived temporarily in an apartment over Mr. Kurts Poole's store. When the house was rebuilt they moved back to the farm. After the passing of Oscar Poole, Darby's brother, Addie and Darby bought Oscar's general merchandise store at Barnesville. They lived in the house across the road and kept the store for several years. Rubin Davis, the youngest son, was born at Barnesville on September 2, 1921.

After a time they moved to Washington and bought a house at 538 - 14th Street, S. E. That was their home for many years until changing neighborhoods made it desirable to move to another location. They then moved to 1611 - 19th Street, S. E. That was where they held their Golden Wedding Anniversary Reception which was attended by a large group of relatives and friends.

Soon after coming to Washington, Darby was employed by the local transportation company which is now known as the D. C. Transit System. He was a Linesman and was subject to call day or night, especially in stormy weather. He never complained about the difficult hours and the work seemed to suit him. He remained in that work until his retirement. Addie worked briefly as a saleslady in a local department store but she was principally a homemaker and mother, rather than a working woman.

As soon as the family was settled in Washington, Addie joined Epworth Methodist Church where she maintained her membership as long as she lived. When attending services became too difficult for her, the minister visited her regularly to talk with her and give her communion.

In addition to her interest in her church, Addie was greatly interested in a patriotic organization of which she was a member, Sons and Daughters of Liberty. She was active in the Lodge for some time and enjoyed the meetings and the social activities.

After Darby's passing on August 24, 1961, Addie continued to live in their home and kept busy and as active as was physically possible until her final illness. She was really incapacitated for just a few weeks and passed away on November 11, 1968 after being hospitalized for about two weeks. She was buried beside Darby in Monocacy Cemetery at Beallsville, Maryland.

The youngest child, William Albert Davis lived for a very short time, and is buried in the Southern Methodist Church Cemetery at Goshen, Maryland.

The Davis Family Reunions

The first Reunion of the John Samuel Davis descendants was held in September 1961 at the Gaithersburg Agricultural Center. No account was kept of the attendance in '61 or '62. But in 1963 more than 100 members attended.

In 1965, the fifth annual reunion was held at the Homewood Capital View Recreational Center.

In 1968 they moved to the Argyle Recreation Center.

The attendance has been as follows:

Year	Attendance
1963	102
1964	80
1965	72
1966	60
1967	74
1968	55

	CH	BORN	MARRIED	DIED
I. Martha Virginia Davis		2-25-1861		10-15-25
I. Margaret Ann Davis	2	7- 7-1862		3-12-01
m. William Bennett		10-27-1851		12- 1-06
A. John Henry Bennett	1	9-15-1882	1909	8- 1-27
m. Flora Riggs		5-10-1892	1909	2-5-73
1. Wilmer	1	12-14-1913	8-31-40	
m. Miriam Southern		12-17-1917	8-31-40	
a. John Alan		7- 4-1947		
B. Roger Davis Bennett	1	11- 4-1891	2- 3-20	12-23-22
m. Beulah Mae Jordan		9-29-1902	2- 3-20	
1. Margaret Virginia		3- 5-1922	9-21-43	
m. Joseph T. Murtha		5-12-1913	9-21-43	
a. Karen Murtha Elliott		6- 8-1946	2-10-68	
b. Christine Ann Murtha		4-21-1948		
c. Kathleen Teresa		1-27-1954		
I. Katie Dorsey Davis	1	4-27-1864	10-10-00	2-17-46
m. Oscar Kurts Poole		2- 7-1875	10-10-00	10-21-18
A. Mable Poole	1	2- 4-1904	4- 5-21	5-24-48
m. William H. Walker		8-27-1901	4- 5-21	1-24-62
1. William Oscar		7- 5-1923	10- 4-44	
m. Florence Ackun		7-11-1925	10- 4-44	
a. William Edward		2- -1948		9-20-61
V. John Jefferson Davis		3-30-1866		7-12-1867
V. Marietta Davis	3	2-19-1868	6-22-92	9-19-60
m. Luther Edwin Harper		4- 8-1867	6-22-92	7-18-42
A. Twin boys died a short time after birth.				
B. Elmira Davis Harper	1	9- 7-1896	5-19-23	
m. Leo Everett Deitrich		4-27-1896	5-19-23	11-18-54
1. Robert Lee		11-11-1924		
I. Alverta Davis	7	2-19-1870	8- 1-94	10-20-39
m. Ignatius Ward		3-20-1870	8- 1-94	10-10-37
A. Johnnie Ignatius	1	8- 5-1895	10- 4-28	7-21-63
m. Mary England		3-11-1901	10- 4-28	
1. Churchill England		11-14-1932	5-12-68	
m. Evelyn Ruth Middaugh			5-12-68	
B. Forrest Eddie		12-25-1897		2-20-54

	CH	BORN	MARRIED	DIED
C. Mary Ella	3	9-27-1899	6-28-19	
m. Julius Carl Hamke		11- 6-1897	6-28-19	
1. Jean Carol		6- 8-1926	8-27-49	
m. Paul Edward Sumbheim		5- 3-1924	8-27-49	
a. Carl David		6-20-1958		
2. Victor Lee		3-10-1928	4-11-53	
m. Ardelia Hutchins		1-23-	4-11-53	
a. Karen Lee		2-27-1954		
b. Carl Everett		8-16-1956		
c. Heidi Sue		6-27-1958		
d. Kurt Andrew		3-27-1962		
3. Gretchen Ann		12-16-1935	6- -57	
m. Donald Harry Brierly		5-25-1934	6- -57	
a. Eric Lee		7- 5-1958		
b. Janet Elizabeth		10-18-1960		
c. Lynda Anne		10-24-1963		
D. Percy Wellington	1	10-16-1901	5-29-25	2- 8-69
m. Louise Johnson		11- 9-1904		
1. Jerry Ward		4- 5-1938	10-19-64	
m. Betty Taylor		11- 9		
E. Ada Viola) Twins				
F. Iva Violet)		3- 3-1904		
G. Alverta Davis	5	11-11-1913	11- 7-32	
m. Eugene Selby		5-15-1909	11- 7-32	12-23-65
1. William Eugene		11-15-1933	1-27-55	
m. Dianne Dupe		10- 6-1935	1-27-55	
a. Jack David		8- 6-1956		
b. Timmy Micky		11- 1-1957		
c. Scott Andrew		4-19-1961		
d. Patrick Steven		7- 6-1962		
e. Eric Mattrews		4-17-1966		
2. Nancy Lee		3- 3-1935	3- 5-54	
m. William Wilkerson		12-16-1927	3- 5-54	
a. Debra Lee		3-17-1958		
b. Pamela Ann Wilkerson		3-25-1961		
c. Bonnie Sue		9- 6-1967		
3. Elizabeth Ann		5-25-1938	9-27-58	
m. James Young		3-10-1933	9-27-58	
a. James Walter Young		5-20-1959		
b. David Eugene		5-25-1961		
4. Bonnie) Twins		7- 6-1951		
5. Charles Thomas)		7- 6-1951		
VII. Emma Augusta Davis	7	11-30-1871	10-16-95	12- -33
m. James Mordecai Purdum		1-26-1870	10-16-95	27
A. Mary Jane	4	8-16-1896	18	8-13-77
m^1. Albert Bowie Allnut		6-21-1896	18	
1. Albert Bowie, Jr.		1- 4-1919	12-27-40	
m^1. Helen Louise Plummer	1	12-27-1940	1-26-22	
a. Patricia Ann		10- 3-1943		

	CH	BORN	MRRIED	DIED
m^2. Doris L. Baker		10-22-1922	7- 8-46	
a. Albert Bowie III		1-17-1949		
b. Robin Sue		4-27-1951		
2. James Purdum Allnut		5-13-1921	6-15-46	
m. Doris J. Brown		3-12-1920		
a. Lawrence Edward		10-14-1948		
b. Robert Wayne		8-29-1952		
3. Dorothy Virginia Allnut		9-18-1922	10-26-44	
m^1. Howard D. Bennett		11-26-1920	10-26-44	
a. Barbara Lee		3- 1-1946	10- 2-65	
m. Thomas Musser, Jr.		4- 6-1944	10- 2-65	
a^1. Thomas Musser III		7-23-1967		
m^2. Joe Grady O'Neal		6-30-1921	9-26-52	
a. Joe Grady II		7- 1-1953		
4. Henry Douglas		2-21-1924	11-22-46	
m. Dorothy Ann Cleveland		7-21-1926	11-22-46	
a. James Douglas		11- 1-1947		
b. Ann Marie		5- 6-1950		
c. Reginald Alan		10-25-1952		
d. Raymond Michael		7-16-1963		
m^2. Perry E. Wallich		11-17-1904	1-18-39	12-21-43
E. James Elliott	4	3-21-1898		
m. Dora E. Johnson		2-17-1899		10- 8-67
1. Mary Virginia	1	8-28-1919		
m^1. Julian W. Brown		4-14-1918	9- 2-37	
a. James Richard		10-19-1940	4-11-66	
m^1. Carolyn Deloris Davidson		4-30-1948		
m^2. Robert Lee Foster		7-18-1921		
a. Mary Virginia				
m^3. Hayward Fergerson		12- 1-1929	7- 4-69	
a. Mary Virginia				
2. Grace E. Purdum		11-17-1929	8-14-41	
m^1. J. Franklin Hastings		7-16-1921		
a. John Franklin		10- 3-1946	5-8-65	
m^1. Gloria Sterling		11-14-1946	5-8-65	
a^1. John Franklin		8- 1-1966		
b^1. Tricia Dawn		12- 3-1968		
b. Jo Ann Hastings		8- 8-1949	7-12-69	
m^1. Robert Lee Richmond		6-16-1947	7-12-69	
m^2. Darrell Dean Halbert		4- 3-1939		
3. James Ray Purdum	3	10-27-1923	8-10-27	
m. Lois N. Moxley		12-10-1927	8-10-27	
a. David R. Purdum		5-19-1948	8-30-69	
m. Evelyn Offutt		1-25-1948	8-30-69	
b. Sharon Gay Purdum		9-30-1955		
c. Lynn Purdum		1-10-1958		
4. Roger Lee		5-25-1926	5-13-50	
m. Evelyn J. Roberts		12-21-1925	5-13-50	
a. Gail Evelyn		3- 1-1951		
b. Ronald Roger		9-20-1956		

	CH	BORN	MARRIED	DIED
C. Maude Virginia	1	11- 9-1900	2- 8-22	9-14-48
m. Jessie C. Burns		11- 9-1903	2- 8-22	4- 3-61
1. Virginia Lou		4-16-1923	4-10-48	
m. John E. Onyun		6-25-1916	4-10-48	
a. John C.		6-10-1954		
D. Maurice Edwin	2	2-24-1903	5-23-23	7- 3-25
m. Julia E. Watkins		11- 5-1903	5-23-23	
1. Maurice Edwin, Jr.		3-10-1925	10-17-48	
m. Katherine V. Waters		4- 7-1930	10-17-48	
a. Elizabeth Ann		3- 9-1950		
b. John Maurice		4- 8-1952		
c. Katherine Lynn		7-10-1957		
d. Mary Susan		7-29-1961		
2. Bertie Louise Purdum		2-12-1924	6- -42	
m. Walter F. Pickett		2-13-1923	6- -42	
a. Walter Marlin		7- 8-1943		
b. Dennis Roger		10- 6-1952		
E. Harry Lee Purdum		6-21-1906	4-27-51	1 - 1
m. Dora Johnson Purdum		2-17-1899	4-27-51	10- 8-67
F. Bessie Eleanor		9-14-1908	4- 1-36	
m. Archie R. Brown		4-22-1906	4- 1-36	
1. Shirley Ann		2-19-1937		
G. Edith Estelle		12-20-1914	4- 7-34	
m. James F. Mullinix		8-22-1910	4- 7-34	
1. Mary Jane		12-23-1937	5-30-59	
m. Maynard Watkins, Jr.		4- 7-1928	5-30-59	
a. Craig Stephen		5- 4-1961		
2. James Kenneth		3-31-1940	9- 1-61	
m. Linda K. Burdette		5-23-1943		
a. Chad Alan		7-22-1962		
VIII. Lillian Davis		4-25-1873		8-10-73
IX. Laura May Davis	2	6-22-1874		1-28-63
m^1. Joseph Purdum		3-24-1875		7-10-13
A. Rufus Davis Purdum	1	2- 2-1898		-23
m. Bessie Berg				
1. George Rufus		2-22-1921		11- 7-22
B. Marietta		1- 9-1909		1- 9-09
m^2. Benjamin C. Hughes		1854		1942

	CH	BORN	MARRIED	DIED
Johanna Davis	6	10- 7-1876	10- 7-99	2-11-42
m. Robert Hays Bowman		7-28-1876	10- 7-99	1- 8-39
A. Mary Frances		11-30-1900	8- 5-33	9-26-7
m. Stanley Gillis Moyer		2- 2-1903	8- 5-33	
B. Robert Jefferson	4	3- 3-1903	6-19-26	
m. Florena Belle Henderson		4-20-1907	6-19-26	
1. Florena Mae		8-20-1927	5- 4-47	
m. Theodore W. Miles		4-17-1918	5- 4-47	
a. Linda Jean		5- 3-1948		
b. Bonnie Mae		11-18-1951		
2. James Robert		8-15-1929		8- 8-42
3. Edna Louise		1-30-1933	8-16-51	
m. David Emerson Kreh		12-28-1930	8-16-51	
a. David Emerson, Jr.		10- 7-1952		
b. Robert Paul		4-18-1954		
c. Julie Ann		10- 2-1961		
d. Gary Veirs		10- 6-1967		
4. Naomi Ruth		11-23-1934	6-22-57	
m. Millard Brown		9-27-1934	6-22-57	
a. Kevin Millard		6- 6-1958		
b. Pamela Naomi		2- 6-1962		
c. Marc Bowman		12-20-1965		
C. Laura Virginia	2	6-18-1905	8- 8-31	10-14-60
m. John Ambrose Moyer		8- 3-1902	8- 8-31	
1. Geraldine		4-27-1934	6-18-54	
m^1. William Warner Soper		4-24-1934	6-18-54	
a. Barbara Ann				
m^2. Robert Gentry		8-15-1921	9-17-66	
2. Mary Ann		12- 5-1940		12- 6-40
D. James Davis Bowman		2- 2-1911	7- 5-31	10-4-71
m^1. Hazel Elizabeth Newcomb				
1. Ann Elizabeth		5- 5-1932	8-16-50	
m. Charles Lancaster			8-16-50	
a. David Dwight		3-25-1952		
m^2. Ethel Moyer		2-22-1916	3-27-41	
2. Delores Louise		11- 1-1941	7-20-57	
m. Kenneth Eugene Trent		12- 3-1938	7-20-57	
a. Lewis Eugene		11-11-1957		
b. June Elaine		12- 2-1958		
c. Donna Louise		7- 2-1962		
d. Wanda Gayle		10-15-1963		
e. Sandra Jane		2- 2-1966		
3. Ethel Elaine		9- 4-1942	10-29-60	
m. Byron Lee Zurnbrun		12- 7-1939	10-29-60	
a. Teresa Elaine		8-17-1961		
b. Byron Lee, Jr.		12-15-1966		
4. James Davis Bowman, Jr.		6-16-1944	12-21-65	
m. Ingrid				
5. Carl Robert		6-10-1945		
6. Alice Gertrude		4-11-1947	7- 9-66	
m. Elwood Ness		9- 4-1937	7- 9-66	
a. Elwood Carlton Ness		11- 4-1967		

	CH	BORN	MARRIED	DIED
E. Ruth Harper		9-14-1913	3-20-39	5-11-60
m. George Riffle Payne		7- 5-1885	3-20-39	5-27-60
F. Anna Bowman		1-28-1920	2-22-42	3-23-68
m. Hugh Edward Williams		9-27-1901	2-22-42	
*XI. Bessie Ellen Davis	6	11-29-1879	4-26-99	7-18-57
m. Hezekiah Barber		7- 6-1875	4-26-99	10-12-57
A. Virginia Ellen		1-27-1899		8-15-01
B. William Edward Barber	1	7-19-1902	9- 5-25	
m. Emily Frances Coates		10-10-1900	9- 5-25	
1. Mary Ellen		12-14-1934	4-11-53	
m. James Wallace Bequette		6-17-1931	4-11-53	
a. Michale Murphy		9-27-1954		
b. Patricia Ellen		12-19-1957		
c. Linda Sue		8-28-1960		
C. John Albert Barber	1	10-11-1904	5-30-30	
m. Marion Agnes Bowling		1-23-1909	5-30-30	
1. Raymond Albert		11-30-1932	6- 6-59	
m. Jean Mildred Small		5-24-1932	6- 6-59	
a. Vanessa Ellen		4- 5-1961		
D. Eva Maude	3	2- 9-1908	12-10-24	
m. Harold Edward Burdette		2- 1-1905	12-10-24	
1. Margaret Elizabeth		8- 3-1927	10-26-46	
m. Downey Monroe Duvall		8-25-1921	10-26-46	
a. Baby Duvall		4- 4-1952		4- 4-52
b. Joan Marill		4-24-1953		
c. James Monroe		6- 4-1955		
d. Donna Jeanne		3-26-1958		
*2. John Edward Burdette		9-12-1932	6-20-51	
m. Barbara Ann		10- 3-1933	6-20-51	
a. Brenda Ann		4-12-1952		
b. Vivian Dianne		9-24-1953		
c. Jacqueline Kay		9- 1-1957		
d. Dale Curtis		9-24-1959		
e. Timothy Edward		11- 6-1963		
3. Glen Harold		5- 7-1947	8- 2-68	
m. Ellen Montgomery		10-11-1949	8- 2-68	
E. Patrick Hezekiah		11- 4-1913	10-18-40	
m. Alice June Perrin		6-16-1917	10-18-40	
a. Sharon June		6-14-1943	6- 3-62	
m. Norlyn Ray Betzer			6- 3-62	
a^1. Tammy Sue		9-13-1963		
b^1. Michael Rae		5-29-1966		
c^1. Scott Rae		4-29-1969		
b. Susan Ellen		4-29-1949		
F. Carlton		8-18-1918		8-19-18

		CH	BORN	MARRIED	DIED
XII.	Eva Maude Davis	1	12- 1-1882	8-17-09	69
	m. Olin Austin Walter		2- 9-1886	8-17-09	2-24-50
A.	Helen Louise Walter		1-19-1911	3-20-43	
	m. Thomas W. Blevins		8-18-1901	3-20-43	
XIII.	Adaline Gartside Davis	3	3- 3-1887	12-20-06	11-11-68
	m. Reginald Darby Poole		10-11-1883	12-20-06	8-24-61
A.	Reginald Leroy	6	10- 6-1907	5-30-27	
	m. Evelyn Loretta Campbell			5-30-27	
	1. Baby Girl		4-17-1928		4-19-28
	2. Barbara Joyce		2- 4-1931	8- 8-48	
	m. David Lee Liggan			8- 8-48	
	a. David Craig Liggan		1- 3-1955		
	3. Donald Leroy Poole			8-15-58	
	m. Catherine Ann Bowling			8-15-58	
	a. Donald Leroy, Jr.		4-30-1959		
	b. Sharron Lynn		10- 4-1961		
	d. Richard Allen				
	4. William Darby Poole		8-28-1938	8-15-64	
	m. Elizabeth Irene Murincsak			8-15-64	
	a. Mary Elizabeth		12-31-1966		
	5. Carolyn Ann		3-15-1944	8-13-63	
	m. Lloyd Thomas Whitaker			8-13-63	
	a. Troy Edward		1- 8-1963		
	b. Thomas David		4- 1-1965		
	c. Barbara Donari		2- 1-1968		
	d. Lloyd Thomas, Jr.		1-20-1969		
	6. Kenneth Wayne		3-31-1969		
B.	Olin Darby Poole		10-15-1910	11- 2-30	
	m. Elsie Alexander			11- 2-30	
	1. Olin Darby II		6-17-1934	10-24-52	
	m. Helen Gardner			10-24-52	
	a. Margo Elizabeth		7-10-1953		
	2. Ronald Glenn		3-21-1938	1-25-69	
	m. Jeanette Marie Olczak			1-25-69	
C.	Rubin Davis Poole		9- 2-1921	12-12-46	
	m. Margaret Elizabeth Gladman			12-12-46	
	1. Robert Davis		11-18-1947	4-12-69	
	m. Melba Lou Howell			4-12-69	
	2. Nancy Lee		7-10-1950		
XIV.	William Albert Davis		4-21-1887	8- 7-87	

This material has been gathered from many sources. Any errors are unintentional.

Elmira Davis Harper Deitrich

September 1969

FOX LAIR

Fox Lair is located on Fox Lair Road. The home was originally named Locust Grove; it was built in the early 1800's, and was the home of Zechariah Macubbin Waters, the Elder.

Zechariah (often called Mac) was born January 15, 1833 to Nathaniel Magruder Waters and Achsah Dorsey. His grandparents were William Waters Jr. and Susannah Magruder (daughter of Col. Zadok Magruder), and Harry Woodward Dorsey and Mary Macubbin, of Sycamore Hollow.

According to Waters' family history, a William Waters lived on 299 acres in Germantown in 1789.

Courtesy of Joyce Hawkins   *Foxlair*

Gladys King History, Goshen Homemakers Club

Waters Family History MCHS

Woodbourne Quilt, MCHS

Self

GOSHEN MANOR

This home was remodeled by Joseph F. Burrows Sr. in the mid 1950's. It was originally a typical farmhouse of the area, and was previously owned by the English and Magruder families. Goshen Manor is located just past Fertile Meadows on Brink Road heading towards Laytonsville, Md. This lovely property has been the site of many fox hunts in the past.

Photo by Richard F. Boggs — Goshen Manor

Mrs. Joseph F. Burrows, oral history

Self

GREEN HILLS FARM

This farmhouse and property had been in the Riggs family for three generations, even though the surrounding properties had been owned by family ancestors five generations ago. On August 14, 1987, the farm which was owned by the four daughters of R. D. Riggs, was sold for development. Fortunately, the farmhouse remains, and is located on Huntmaster Road.

For many years Green Hills Farm was a large Holstein dairy farm in Goshen. In the 1970's and 1980's, it was a common sight to see a profusion of black and white cows grazing near the creek bed and old mill sites that once contributed to Goshen's prosperity. The house was built in the 1880's, shortly after Harry Riggs purchased the property from David and Mary Peugh (Pugh) in 1881. The Peughs had an earlier home on the property. The present home is a 2 1/2 story ell-shaped frame house with a tin roof. A wing was added in 1960. The original barn at Green Hills had a fieldstone foundation with hand-hewn beams and uprights. Farms like this that were scattered throughout the Goshen area were totally self sufficient. Because of the abundant source of labor, there was no chore too difficult to be done on the farm as long as one could pay for the service. On Green Hills farm, hog butchering was done during the first week in December for three days: Monday through Wednesday. The farmer's wife brought in hired help for the household duties during this time. There was much to do: sausages had to be made and hams had to be hung in the smokehouse. Fortunately, she could afford the outside help.

Harry was the son of Remus D. Riggs of Fertile Meadows and grandson of George Washington Riggs, the first Riggs to own "Fertile Meadows." Harry began his dairy farm with "mixed breeds." It was his son R. D. Riggs who then switched to regular Holstein cattle. R. D. Riggs was one of the original members of the Maryland & Virginia Milk Producers Association. He received a pin for 50 years of continuous milk shipments to Washington D. C.

This farm was the site of many fox hunts over the years. Today, lovely new homes are springing up on the meadow land, slowly changing the bucolic landscape.

The four daughters of R.D. Riggs are: Hazel Liggon, Mary Lou Stinson, Joyce Hawkins and Barbara Anne Stiles.

Courtesy of Joyce Hawkins   Green Hills Farm

Green Hills Farm

Montgomery County Historical Society

Gladys King History; Goshen Homemakers Club

Joyce Hawkins, oral history

Mary Lou Stinson, oral history

Charles Burton, oral history

Self

Somerset Orme Jones Farm

SOMERSET ORME JONES FARM
LOCHAVEN DRIVE

Somerset, son of John Jones of "Goshen House" (later renamed to "Honeysuckle Hill"), bought out the family heirs of this farm, and took over management around the 1860's. The farmhouse was built about 1850 with the extension added a short time later. Somerset referred to this place as "Kildeer Park". He put tenants in the house but visited daily to oversee the farming as he remained living at the family home "Goshen House".

Somerset was a lifelong bachelor, who was elected to the Maryland House of Delegates in 1875 and 1883 on the Democratic ticket. While serving on the legislature, he was a member of the state agriculture committee. He was one of the founders of the First National Bank of Gaithersburg, which opened for business on or about September 1, 1891. He served on the building committee of "Old Goshen" Methodist Church.

This home was left to a sister of Somerset (Nannie) who married Daniel Chambers. The farm later became known as "Old Judge Chambers" place. He lived in Baltimore and used the farm as a summer home. During his ownership, asparagus, strawberries, and watercress were grown here. In later years, the farm fell into the hands of Whitaker Chambers, who accused Alger Hiss of being a communist before the House Un-American Activities Committee.

In 1949, the farm was purchased by William Fulks; later, Ed Mayne acquired this farm and began restoration. Next, the Richard Allen family purchased it and completed the restoration. Many other families have enjoyed ownership of this home in recent years. The surrounding property has become the m, n, and p sections of Goshen Estates. The slate roofed, log corn crib that was once part of this farm was donated to the Montgomery County Fairgrounds by Ed Mayne in August of 1976.

Jones log corn-crib moved to fairgrounds

GAITHERSBURG — The Somerset Jones log corn-crib was moved to the Montgomery County Fairgrounds Aug. 9 in preparation for the fair which opens next Monday.

The building was located on the old Somerset Jones farm at Goshen, north of Gaithersburg. Although the structure is a rare survivor of its type, the construction methods are typical of those used on early log buildings in the County. The massive, hand-hewn log walls (mostly of oak, but some may be chestnut) are squared and joined at the corners with V-shaped notches.

In other log buildings the spaces between the logs were usually filled with stones and clay. However, due to the fact that this was used for many years as a corn crib, the spaces were only partially-filled in by split boards — which kept rodents out, but allowed the air through to dry the corn. In addition, the corn was protected by a rough, split-oak floor and a stone pier foundation. The building was also used as a smokehouse at one time.

Slate Roof

Perhaps the most unusual feature of the structure is the fact that it has a slate roof. Only two other log buildings in the county were known to have had slate roofs, and these were both dwellings. While the roof appears to be a replacement for the original (a common repair) it still probably dates at least to the turn-of-the-century, and it is believed that the slate was a local product obtained from a quarry at Hyattstown, near Sugarloaf Mountain.

The building is over 100 years old, and very possibly dates to the early 19th century. The Jones family settled about 1800, at a time when the Goshen Mills were established along a new road that linked the county with the Baltimore grain markets. Their ancestors had originally settled in the county in the 1700's along Cabin John Creek, near the present-day Montgomery Mall area.

The man who made most of the improvements to the farm was Somerset Orme Jones, who was born in 1835 and died in 1914. He had assumed ownership and management of the farm by the 1860's — after his parents had died, and most of his brothers and sisters had married or moved away.

Jones himself was a life-long bachelor, who worked hard and greatly improved the value of the farm. In addition to his success at farming, he was also active in community religious, business, and political affairs.

He was on the building committee of the Goshen Methodist Episcopal Church-South (now the Mennonite Church), and was a founder of the First National Bank of Gaithersburg. He was elected to the Maryland House of Delegates in 1875 and 1883. During his service with the legislature, he was a member of the state agricultural committee.

Courtesy of The Gaithersburg Gazette

Jones Corn-Crib

Somerset Orme Jones Farm

Richard Allen Family

County Courier, Aug. 18, 1976

Gladys King History; Goshen Homakers Club

Memories of Katherine Riggs Poole; Nov. 1969, Montgomery Historical Society

People and Places and Pot Pourri by Jacobs Malloy.

Self

OAKHURST

Oakhurst is located at the end of Huntmaster Drive. This was the home of Zechariah McCubbin Waters, the younger. It has a very early log home on the property, originally used as slave quarters. It has been converted into a guest house. At one time there was a breathtaking view of the Seneca Valley from this location. Now there are many homes dotting the landscape.

Courtesy of Joyce Hawkins   *Oakhurst*

Gladys King History, Goshen Homemakers Club

Self

OLD GOSHEN METHODIST CHURCH
by Ella Plummer - 1962

"On the road between Laytonsville and Gaithersburg there stands today an interesting brick church amid a grove of stately oak trees.

"On this site sometime before 1790, a group of local Methodists erected a log church. Formal deed to the land was given in 1790 by Ignatius Pigman. In an earlier deed from Pigman to adjoining property, Pigman refers to a church already in existence there.

"The little log church was very plain in appearance - no plaster on the walls - no underdrawing - no painting or decorating of any kind. In those days more attention was paid to utility than to beauty. The benches were made of just one plank without backrests.

"Fancy if you can a person accustomed to sitting in one of our comfortably cushioned pews, sitting on one of those rough benches patiently listening to, and evidently enjoying a sermon an hour and a half long from the text, 'Endure hardness as a good soldier'.

"The floor was boarded and somewhere there was a bad place, for it is said that Mrs. Wilson, a nervous lady, accidentally went through - the scene may be better imagined than described.

"The pulpit was a very tall narrow box elevated some three or four steps from the ground. Early pulpits were built high, so that when the minister sat down he might have a moment's relief from the searching gaze of his congregation. It also offered a place of seclusion to which he could repair after a long journey on horseback and arrange any repairs needed for presenting a neat appearance.

"It also gave the minister an opportunity of finding out how the congregation behaved in his absence. On one occasion when the minister had taken refuge in his pulpit before any of the congregation knew he was there, the people gathering in the church were engaged in conversation and laughter. Suddenly a deep and solemn voice was heard saying, 'The Lord is in His Holy Temple, let all the earth keep silence before him'.

"One minister of the old log church was a Mr. Jones from England who studied for the Catholic priesthood. Coming to accept a church in Washington, he stopped at a revival service of the Methodists, was converted, and entered the Ministry to win great fame as a brilliant orator.

Old Goshen Methodist Church

"Among early members of the log church were Dr. Richard Waters, a surgeon in the Revolution and his wife Mrs. Margaret Smith Waters. Richard Waters, jr., better known as 'Uncle Dicky' taught school in the old log meeting house. He joined the Church late in life and was always a great inspiration to the minister. He lived to be over ninety.

"This is about all that is known of the little log Church which held a warm place in the hearts of its worshipers. But when they became prosperous, they felt it was not worthy of God if the congregation could afford a better Church. So, in 1830, they decided to build a brick church.

"Led by Father James Paynter the spirit of improvement rapidly spread and soon took practical shape in the starting of a brick kiln in the field across the road from the Church, the brick maker being a Mr. Ray.

"By 1830 the building was completed. It stood near the road on the site of the old Meeting House, the door facing the present Church, but had no vestibule. Broad stone steps led up to the three doors of entrance, one of which opened into the ladies' aisle, one into the gentlemen's, and the third into the gallery over the rear of the Church where the slaves who came with their masters could sit.

"The pulpit was high and boxed - the preacher could be seen only when standing; the walls were whitewashed and there were no stained glass windows. A partition just high enough for the boys to peep over divided the men from the fairer sex and the whole was kept comfortable by two large stoves. To our minds this seems a plain, unpretentious building but then it was considered a unique and beautiful edifice.

"The person chiefly responsible for the building of this temple of elegant proportions was Father James Paynter. The memory of this good man, a zealous Methodist, should be ever kept green. The stone covering his grave in the grove in front of the present Church carries his epitaph - 'born Sept. 1, 1764 in Sussex, Delaware and fell asleep in Christ March 1, 1840. He entered the itinerant ministry of the M. E. Church in 1792 and continued a devoted and useful member until death.' An itinerant until the later years of his life when he located at Goshen, he took a deep interest in everything that concerned the Church, helped with his own hands in building it and was so particular about keeping the interior clean, that it was his habit to ask the congregation to wipe their feet before entering its doors, and he never failed to back this precept by his own vigorous example. So dear to his heart was the Church, that he requested that his body be buried at the back of the pulpit, which was done.

"James Paynter's will is in Rockville. It was probated in 1840 and stated: 'I James Paynter as Elder in the Methodist Episcopal Church of the United States of America and a member of the Baltimore

Old Goshen Methodist Church

Annual Conference do hereby leave to my friend, Benjamin Lyon, $50 in cash, my horse, saddle and bridle, my saddle-bags, and my trunk, my watch and all my books and wearing apparel. If he should die, his widow shall heir and claim under this will, all except my wearing apparel, which I then leave to the needy.'

"Obviously it is not possible to name all who have served Goshen Church as pastors or to mention those who have worshiped in its three buildings. Taking a sampling of names found in the Records, it will be seen that there is a remarkable continuity of family names. In 1853, for instance, trustees of the Church were Jefferson Griffith, William Thompson of R., M.L. Pugh, Uriah H. Griffith, William H. Waters, D.L. Pugh, J.F.D. Magruder, Richard Green and Jonathan Dudley. Any later sampling would include many of the same family names.

"In 1860 came the stormy period of the Civil War. Services were held but some of the bitter feeling engendered by the strife crept into the Church and caused the only schism that has ever marred the history of the Goshen Church. The majority of the members sympathized with the M.E. Church South, but as both of the M.E. Church South and the M.E. Church North laid claim to the property the case was carried into Court and resulted in favor of the M.E. Church North.

"At this point Mr. William Thompson of R. purchased the Church building with the grove around it for $500 and presented it back to the M.E. Church South.

"By 1869, the old brick walls that had echoed many an eloquent sermon and repeated songs of praise had become weak and unsafe. The Congregation was compelled to worship in the Schoolhouse.

"Accordingly the old building was torn down and the good bricks were added to the new ones to erect a new Church begun in the Fall of 1870. The architect was Walter West of Washington, D.C. who gave his services; the master builder was S.G. Henseley; and his assistant was Mr. Lee. The bricklayer was a Mr. Jones who presented the Church with a handsome large Bible.

"Interesting features of the present Church include two handsome chandeliers. The one in front was bought at the time the present Church was built in 1870. The one toward the back came from the second Church. The balcony is or was reached from the outside and has a folding door. The bottom step is concave to allow the door to be pushed and folded.

"Many anecdotes are told of olden times in the Churches. About the time of the Civil War the Sunday School Superintendent noted one Sunday: 'a small attendance; the boys are in the cherry trees and refuse to come down'. On one occasion a horse refused to pass the Church Cemetery and ghosts were suspected; however, the intrepid driver finally conquered his fears and got out to investigate and

Old Goshen Methodist Church

found a cow lying in the road! During service on another occasion a long black snake dropped from the balcony into a lady's lap.

"At the time of the dedication of the Third Church in 1871, there were living several members who had worshiped in all three Churches. Among them were: 'Uncle' Dicky Waters, Miss Charlotte Waters, Mrs. Elizabeth Cooke, Mrs. Emiline Stewart and Mrs. William Thompson of R.

"Names associated with 'Old Goshen" run nearly the whole alphabet, some of them being: Allnutt, Balthis, Bowman, Butcher, Benson, Cooke, Carter, Clagett, Crawford, Dorsey, Davis, Eggleston, Gartner, Green, Gaither, Griffith, Higgins, Haines, Harmon, Jones, Kinsey, Kephart, Linthicum, Martin, Magruder, Moore, Moxley, Mariweather, Nelson, Pope, Plummer, Pumphrey, Pugh, Riggs, Stewart, Stupp, Tompson, Waters, Watson, White, Williams, Warfield, Walker, Wightman.

"The membership of Goshen Church decreased through the years by removals and deaths. When the Nothern and Southern Methodists, who had separated during the Civil War, decided to unite with the Methodist Protestants, it seemed more logical to keep Church activities in the village of Laytonsville. The Church there became the successor to Goshen Church which was closed as a place of worship for the Methodist denomination. At the time this was done a group of Trustees was organized and incorporated. The Church and Cemetery were deeded to these Trustees and not the Conference. In 1950 the Trustees were: Samuel Riggs, George Plummer, Nathan White, Mrs. Maude Cooke, Mrs. Lee Warfield, Miss Maude Dorsey and Miss Ella R. Plummer.

"On December 10, 1950, the old Church was rededicated under the auspices of the Eastern Mennonite Board of Missions and Charities to whom it was leased. The only consideration is that the Mennonites keep up the Church property and take care of the Cemetery.

"Thus the worship of God continues in the Church which, as the successor of two earlier Churches, is a sacred spot in the minds of many whose memories include services there, and in the minds of many others whose forbears worshiped there and are buried there."

AUTHOR'S NOTE

As of this writing, "Old Goshen" is no longer owned by the Methodist Church. A group of local citizens called "The Cemetery Committee" now owns the property. The Mennonites still lease the church from this committee.

Courtesy of The Sentinel Montgomery County

THE SENTINEL MONTGOMERY COUNTY Thursday, September 30, 1976 B-19

Goshen Church: Original, log structure was torn down.
Sentinel Photo by Staff Photographer Carol Woods

Courtesy of Ardith Gunderman Boggs

Old Goshen Methodist Church

Ella Plummer, The Montgomery County Story, MCHS November, 1962

Self

IGNATIUS PIGMAN

Ignatius Pigman was the fourth child and the third son of five children born to Matthew and Mary Pigman in 1755 near Laytonsville, Maryland, on property titled "Upper Newfoundland Hundred." In 1760, Matthew married for a second time to Dorcus Gartrell. It appears his children were of his first wife Mary.

In 1778, Matthew signed the Oath of Fidelity. The following year, he was appointed "Overseer" for selected roads by the county. This position meant he was responsible for the general upkeep of the roads. In 1783, he had three slaves and three whites on 980 acres in Laytonsville. Matthew is also credited with founding Damascus, Maryland. By the following year, on June 28, his will was probated. His other children were: sons John and Joshua, and daughters Philenia and Sarah. The daughters moved to Kentucky when they became adults.

Ignatius was a minister, adventurer, opportunist and holder of thousands of acres. In spite of this, he is said to have died in poverty. When he was twenty years old, he received 122 acres in Anne Arundel County, which was the site of a Pigman Mill. In 1777, on August 3, Ignatius married Suzannah Lamar. The years that followed were filled with his work in ministry with the Methodist church. In 1781, he was assigned by the Baltimore Conference to the Berkeley Circuit. Since there were very few church buildings or meeting houses that early, most of the preaching took place in private homes. Berkeley Circuit was a far-ranging circuit that centered around Berkeley County, West Virginia and Virginia. It probably took Ignatius more than a week to complete. In 1782, he was sent to Fairfax, Virginia. By 1783, he was assigned to Frederick, Maryland. He was sent to St. Mary's Circuit in 1785.

Before 1784, Methodist ministers were all laymen who were licensed to preach. These ministers were not ordained and therefore could not administer the three sacraments: Baptism, Communion, and Marriage. After the American Revolution, and the subsequent political separation from England, John Wesley deemed it advisable to establish a separate church and ordain the preachers so that they could provide all the sacraments. At the Christmas Conference in 1784 at Baltimore, 60 of the 83 preachers in America were able to attend. They voted to elect Francis Asbury as their General Superintendent and to establish the Methodist Episcopal Church. Ignatius Pigman is said to have been elected a deacon at this meeting, and ordained an elder in April, 1785, thus giving him the right to perform all duties of ordained clergy.   Presiding

Ignatius Pigman

Elders (the original title of District Superintendents) were supervising clergy over a number of others and presided at quarterly meetings of the circuits. Ignatius was a Presiding Elder over Baltimore, Frederick, and Calvert Counties. In 1788, he received partial location and support from the conference. Location meant that a traveling preacher who was salaried and under appointment by the Conference, ceased to travel. He may have continued his ministry on a voluntary unpaid basis. This was usually because of health, family or business reasons. Ignatius received partial location which probably meant he still received partial salary for his duties other than traveling.

In the late 1780's Ignatius sold a plot of land for five shillings for the first Methodist Church in Goshen. The deed was formalized in 1790. There were many land transactions between Ignatius and his brother Joshua, and Ed Crow. They built many mills including the Goshen Mills, and one as far south as Georgetown.

Ignatius was first among the most esteemed of eloquent preachers. When he became disenchanted after six years, there was much grief among his following when he abandoned his position. Circuit riding and low pay rekindled his love for real estate. He began to travel to Kentucky and bought land there. He traveled back and forth between Maryland and Kentucky, luring Montgomery Countians to Ohio County, Kentucky to buy land.

Ignatius's Revolutionary War records state: Methodist preacher, draughted, delinquent. By 1792, he was County Roads Commissioner living in the fourth district.

A few years later, Bishop Asbury was traveling in the Clarksburg area of Montgomery County and wrote the following in his journal: "1 Sept. 1800 (Monday) - We hobbled along to Clarksburg. On the way we dined at Joshua Pigmans'. Here I once more saw his brother Ignatius. Art thou he? Ah but O how fallen! How changed from how I knew thee once! Lord, what is man if left to himself?"

Many who followed Ignatius to Kentucky became angry with him when they found that the land they purchased often became flooded by the Ohio River. Ignatius built several churches; the one in Goshen was an early one. He built one in Frederick probably when he was assigned there as a circuit rider. He built one in Kentucky and then went on to New Orleans where he is said to have died around 1812 - 1816 at about 60 years of age, in poverty.

Ignatius and his wife Suzannah Lamar had the following children: Rhoda: born - 1778; Anne (Amy): born - 1781; Sallie: born - 1784; Polly: born - 1790 (died young); Sidney (female): born - 1809; Philenia: born - 1813; Wesley: born - ?. After Ignatius died, Suzannah married a cousin, John Lamar.

Ignatius Pigman

John Pigman & His Descendants, Kelleher, Funk Young & Whitt pp.25-26, MCHS

Gladys King History, Goshen Homemakers Club

History of Goshen Mills and Immediate Area, the Goshen Mills Chapter, NSDAR, MCHS

Commission on Archives and History, Baltimore Conference of the United Methodist Church

John Baines, Park Naturalist, M-NCPPC

GOSHEN SCHOOLS

The first Goshen school was the log church known as Goshen Chapel. This first church was Methodist and the first of three buildings on the site. It was used as a school for the local children as the community grew. The teacher was Richard Waters Jr., son of Dr. Richard Waters of Revolutionary War fame. He was known to the children as "Uncle Dicky" and lived to be over ninety years old. This building was replaced by a brick church in 1830.

The second school was on the southeast corner of route 124 and Goshen Road (now Brink Road). It was listed as the South Public School in the 1879 survey. In a state insurance report of 1868, the school shows 50 pupils and a William H. Pace as teacher. On June 9, 1903, the Montgomery County Sentinel reported that "the public school at Goshen, this county, was destroyed by fire last Tuesday night. All the contents were also consumed. The loss is placed at $500.00; insurance, $290.00." The local people repeat the story of the school children arriving at school one morning only to find the building burned nearly to the ground. Although the school was to be closed for obvious reasons while Laytonsville School was being built, it apparently was restored and used in 1906. At this time the attendance was below minimum. In 1912, a delegation requested that the school in Laytonsville be made a high school, with pupils being transported from Goshen and Claysville. By September 26, 1917, the South Public School was closed for good.

It was a credit to Mr. Pace and the South Public School that the education was said to be excellent. The grandchildren of the Jones family, Annie and Kate Jones, practically lived at "Goshen," just to profit from the fine education offered at the neighborhood school.

The third Goshen school was built on property donated by Harry Riggs for $50.00. It was built on Blunt Road (now Huntmaster Road) located down the hill from Goshen School Road on the right-hand side. Today it is the center section of a little house that was once a tenant house belonging to Green Hills Farm. This was used until 1919 when the children were hauled by horse drawn wagons to the new school located in Laytonsville, Maryland. In 1922, the schoolhouse property was sold back to Riggs of Green Hills Farm for $455.00.

Goshen School Road was named by Harrison King, who recommended the name to the Supervisor of Road Maintenance. In earlier times the children walked along this road to the little Goshen School on Blunt Road (now Huntmaster). Previously, the road was named Davis Mill Road and Log House Road.

Goshen Schools

Today there is a fourth Goshen school located on the corner of Warfield Road and Miracle Drive. It is a modern elementary school serving the Goshen community, Montgomery Village, and the surrounding areas. It is appropriately named Goshen Elementary School.

Courtesy of Joyce Hawkins   *Goshen Schoolhouse*

Third Goshen School

Goshen Schools

Harrison King, oral history

Gladys King History, Goshen Homemakers Club

Schools That Were, (insurance papers), MCHS

Joyce Riggs Hawkins, oral history

Joyce Hawkins, "At Home in Goshen" Newsletters, March & April, 1991

Mary Lou Riggs Stinson, oral history

1887 Survey, MCHS

Self

PRATHERTOWN

In 1883, Moses, Marshall, John, Rezin, and Annie Prather bought about 6 and 1/2 to 7 and 1/2 acres of land in the area of Wightman Road above Montgomery Village, for $60.00 an acre. They paid cash to William H. Benson and his wife Jane for this land that was called "Dorsey's Meadows." Later some adjacent lands were acquired by James and Moses Wilson, Wesley Boyd, and Basel Frazier. This became Prathertown. Many people living there were and are direct descendants of the black slaves from this area. According to Rev. James E. Prather's oral history, Moses Prather was a slave working at the Blunt Farm, but Marshall was not a slave. Reverend Prather's great-grandparents were slaves. His great-grandmother was Hannah Bowie.

At one time Reverend Prather was a businessman in Gaithersburg. He made cement splash blocks and sold them to the builders of the area. He was pressured to move by the other local businesses who needed more space to expand. Finally, he left the Gaithersburg business district, having been the last black businessman in town. Reverend Prather was also active as a part-time minister in the Methodist Church and then later in the Baptist Church.

Today, Prathertown has been surrounded by Montgomery Village and Goshen Estates. However, it remains a pleasant community, reminding those of us who live in this rapidly growing area of days gone by.

Rev. James Prather oral history; "Conversations on a Community" by Andrea Stevens, April 22, 1976 MCHS.

Self

Harrison and Gladys King

HARRISON AND GLADYS KING

In 1914, Harrison King, who was then nearly two years old, moved to the King Farm on Goshen School Road with his family. His father, Charlie Dow King, built the farmhouse the same year and with his wife, Augusta Ward King, began to farm the land. The hen houses, barn and stable were already there, as his first cousin, Storzie King, previously owned and operated the farm. Storzie purchased the farm from Elgie Riggs. Charlie King came to this location from Kingstead Farm in Kings Valley, southwest of Damascus. It is from the Damascus farm that the nationally known "Kingstead Holstein" was bred. This herd was started by Leslie King, brother of Harrison's father Charlie Dow King.

When Harrison became of school age, he attended the brand-new public school in Laytonsville. The Goshen Schoolhouse had closed the year before. The children were taken to school in horse-drawn wagons. This new school had consolidated the little Goshen School and the Claysville School.

At the same time, a little girl named Gladys Allnut began to attend school in Etchison. The Allnuts had moved from Howard County to a small farm in Etchison, a small town north of Laytonsville on Route 108. Gladys and Harrison met while attending high school in Gaithersburg. They were later married and continued their life together on the Goshen Farm. This couple did much to enrich the lives of families in the Goshen area.

Harrison was one of the founders of the Montgomery County Fair. He, with other countians, built many of the fairground buildings, including the cattle barns, dining hall, etc. Harrison and others were honored during ceremonies at the 1992 Montgomery County Fair. The land for the fairgrounds was purchased from Herman Rabbit by the Farm Bureau. The Bureau in turn built the first building which was the Agriculture Center. Harrison remembers that the early fairs consisted of tents until the buildings were constructed. His wife, Gladys, worked with others in the first kitchen, which was in a tent. This was in 1949.

Gladys organized the Woodfield 4H club and turned it over to the local people to operate. She then organized the Goshen 4H Club which has served this community ever since. Hundreds of girls and boys have enjoyed their multiple successes at the Montgomery County Fair due to this club and its organizer. Many parents in turn have become 4H leaders living up to the fine example that Gladys and her family set for them and their children. She also organized the Goshen Homemakers

Club which inspired this "writer" to continue Gladys's work on the history of Goshen.

Harrison suggested the name Goshen School for the road on which his farm was located. He felt this would be a lasting reminder of the days when the Goshen children walked to the little one-room schoolhouse located at its end, around the corner on Huntmaster Road. In those days (the 1930's), people could suggest road names to the Supervisor of Road Maintenance if the former name was no longer valid. The road was previously called Davis Mill Road and sometimes Log House Road. Since there was a Davis Mill Road at the old mill site, the suggestion was accepted. In the late 1800's and early 1900's before the present Goshen School Road was built, Davis Mill Road did cut across the fields from Rt. 124, all the way to John Davis's mill, which was located on the present Davis Mill Road on Wildcat Creek.

In the 1950's, Harrison bought the Copeland farm next door, and restored it. Before the restoration and King ownership, one of the Copeland daughters married Darius Prather. They lived there and raised their family. A grandson of this family, named Thomas Prather, has bestowed on his family the honor of becoming a General in the United States Army.

Although Gladys King died on March 11, 1989, her memory will live on forever. She was everyone's mother and grandmother. She and Harrison provided an opportunity for many children and their parents to visit a working farm, a life style that is rapidly disappearing from the Goshen landscape.

HARRISON KING'S HOUSE

Courtesy of Joyce Hawkins

Harrison and Gladys King

Harrison King, oral history, 1992

Self

Goshen Ghosts

GOSHEN GHOSTS

There is a house down on Wildcat Creek where a bridesmaid burned to death when she smothered the bride's veil, which was ignited accidently by a lantern. The bride was her sister, and their name was Waters. A psychic visited the home and could feel the ghost in the dining room, accompanied by a chilly draft. For a whole month, the owners were awakened at night by the smell of coffee brewing (perhaps by a restless spirit).

The 18th-century home owned for many years by Lee and Brita Counselman, named "Fertile Meadows," was said to have no ghosts. However, Brita did remember a peculiar experience at her place back in the 1930's. When she was alone, she could hear a woman singing in the house. "It was a gentle, old fashioned voice, a bit sad," she said. When the renovations began, the singing woman was driven away, never to return. Rachel Robertson's tombstone is out back beside the tombstone of her husband and some of their children. They were very early owners of "Fertile Meadows." Do you suppose?

"Honeysuckle Hill," formerly called "Goshen House," has been the scene of some ghostly experiences. Because it is said to have stood vacant for about eleven years in the first half of the 1900s, stories began to circulate. The house began to take on a "spooky" appearance. The property also had its very own graveyard where the original family, named Jones, were laid to rest. There was also some mystery about the identity of a young woman named Annie Linthicum, who was buried alongside the Jones family members. Further research has identified her as a granddaughter of the original owner, John Jones. However, in the 1970s, a family who lived in the house did experience several unusual happenings. One morning in November of 1972, after the children had gone to school, the mother was startled by a loud thumping sound behind her. For a moment, she thought someone had fallen down the stairs; then she remembered that she was alone except for her dog and cat. The dog ran up and down the stairs, barking. The cat hissed and the fur stood up on its back. A few minutes later it happened again. When she later related this experience to her husband, he scoffed at her and dismissed it from his mind. A few nights later he was awakened by someone or something grabbing him by the shoulder and shaking him. But when he looked to see who it was, no one was there. After it happened a second time, he became a believer. The following spring, voices were heard in the area of the upstairs hallway. At first the mother incorrectly thought it was a radio. The voices were very faint but in conversation. A woman was crying and a man was trying to comfort her. Everything seemed normal until the next November. Again, the thumping sounds occurred on the stairs. It is known that Emma Jones, the youngest child of John experienced heartbreak when her fiance died in his early twenties. She wanted to marry him on his death bed, but the family did not approve. She never married until she was well into her sixties. Even then, she still wore the ring that was to have been her wedding ring from her lover, and his picture continued to hang above her bed. Her only jewelry was made from a lock of his hair: earrings and a brooch.

One of the strangest ghostly Goshen occurrences happened in the late 1980s. On a January evening, just as a brilliant winter sunset was taking place, a lady was driving her pickup on Brink Road approaching the old Goshen Mennonite Church (formerly Methodist). She frequently passed this church at this time each day because she was returning home from her job as a horse trainer in the Etchison area. She also admitted that "Old Goshen" had always beckoned to her but never understood why. On this particular evening, the church was surrounded by a green glow and she couldn't tear her attention away from it. When she glanced back at the road ahead of her, she saw a black figure with his arms outstretched, motioning for her to stop. She said he wore a black, wide brimmed hat, black coat and pants. He looked to her like a preacher. As she slammed on her brakes and skidded closer to the figure, she saw, to her horror, that his face was a skull and his hands were skeletal bones. He then disappeared. In her rear-view mirror, she saw him holding up his bony hands, stopping the car behind her. She could hear the brakes screeching. At that point, she drove immediately home. She later began to have recurring dreams of an oak leaf. It was rather stylized, so she drew a picture of it. She was told that perhaps she should return to "Old Goshen" and visit the cemetery and grounds. When she did this, she found she was drawn to a large oak tree, but its leaf was not as the leaf appeared in her dream. But, as she looked further, she found a tombstone with the name Waters, and by the name was engraved an oak leaf like the one in her dream. One Zechariah McCubbin Waters, the Elder, of Goshen, named his homestead "The Oaks." What does it all mean? The preacher in the road has been sighted many times over the years. What could have happened to cause such a restless spirit?

The old Windham farmhouse on Delta Court was the site of a tragic event. During the civil war, a soldier was killed in the dining room of this house. This incident left a blood stain on the floor. The Goldens, who owned the farm during the 1950's and 1960's, repeatedly tried to remove this by sanding and other means. However, it kept returning and was said to have stained the rug that covered it as well. On a cold and snowy night, a guest of this family was invited to remain overnight. She was given the small room off the landing of the front staircase. It was known as the maid's quarters and always had a chill associated with it. The guest found that her bed covers were constantly sliding to the floor. No matter what she did, she was unable to prevent the bedding from uncovering her. The next morning the owner admitted to the presence of a female ghost that apparently was having some fun with their overnight guest.

Goshen Ghosts

Gladys King, Goshen History, Goshen Homemakers Club

Oral histories received from local citizens who shall remain anonymous.

Self

WINDHAM FARM

Windham Farm was one of the later farms in the Goshen area and was occupied by the Windham family from 1876 to 1936. After this sixty year occupancy, the Burnhams purchased the farm. Because Mrs. Burnham was very civic minded and active in the Republican Party, she became well known in the area. The local people began to refer to the section of Route 124 where the farm was located as Burnham Road. This part of the road is located between Warfield Road and the Brink Road/Route 124 intersection.

During the 1950's and 1960's, the home was occupied by the Jack Watson Golden family. The lane that led from Route 124 to the farmhouse was lined with apple trees. This lane had replaced a former approach also from Route 124 which had brick posts at the entrance that were crumbling with age. This pathway was overgrown and impassable. During the Golden occupancy, there still remained, on the property, a small stone building that was slightly rounded. It had a dirt floor and a wooden door with an iron barred window. It was believed to have been the slave quarters from earlier days. On this farm, the Goldens operated the Rod/Gar Kennels where they boarded dogs and other animals.

The farmhouse, which was last restored by the Norman Price family, is located on Delta Court in Goshen Estates.

Photo by Richard F. Boggs — *Windham Farm*

Windham Farm

Gladys King, Goshen History, Goshen Homemakers Club

Barbara Mannino, oral history 1993

Self

WOODBOURNE

This is the earliest of the Blunt homes, located on the section of Blunt Road between Brink Road and Route 355. It has been in the Blunt family for five generations. Woodbourne, which was built in 1805, was apparently owned by Henry Woodward Dorsey of Sycamore Hollow. When he died in 1840, he left Woodbourne Estate to his daughter Harriet Dorsey Blunt who had married Samuel Blunt in 1818. Harriet and Harry Woodward Dorsey of Sycamore Hollow, were children of Henry Woodward Dorsey, but had different mothers.

An early room in the top of the dairy was equipped with school desks, as the family children had a private tutor who lived with them in an "ell" that was added on to the back of the house. The central part of the home is the original log cabin, which was bricked over in 1845 from bricks made on the premises. At this time other additions were made. The home included an ice house, dairy house (previously mentioned), and a very rare four-leveled and pegged barn. In its early splendour, Woodbourne was furnished in style with valuable antiques. It had one of the loveliest settings of any of the original homes.

Today Woodbourne is surrounded by encroaching suburbia and has become rundown.

It was in this home that the "Woodbourne Quilt" was made by Harriet Dorsey Blunt and Susan Maria Waters Dorsey in 1852. It has been shown in museums in the Washington and Baltimore area.

Courtesy of The Sentinel Montgomery County

Prather slaves are said to have toiled here at Woodbourne.

Courtesy of Joyce Hawkins   *Woodbourne*

Woodbourne

Gladys King, Goshen History, Goshen Homemakers Club

Mrs. Edward Blunt, oral history

Dorsey/Blunt Genealogy, MCHS

Self

ABOUT THE AUTHOR

When Ardie Boggs and her family moved to Goshen, Maryland over twenty years ago, she heard of a threat by the County to develop a recreational lake, which would endanger many of the historical homes. Some of these homes were opened for tours to convey what would be lost forever if the lake project went through. Fortunately, the flooding of the area was stifled, but Ardie's interest in its history was stirred.

Ardie met Gladys King, a longtime resident who had begun a written history of Goshen. She encouraged Ardie to continue writing it in her stead. Soon thereafter, Ardie began organizing tours of the lovely homes and buildings and also began accepting local speaking engagements about the area's history. Over the years she kept an ever-growing journal of Goshen's past. This made her realize the need for a book to be written which would help preserve the historical qualities of Goshen.

Ardie has many interests including collecting antiques, genealogy, and decorative painting. She plays the Celtic Harp professionally and has published a book of her original music for the harp titled, "Celtic Whispers."

The Boggs family includes her husband Dick, two children and two grandchildren.

www.ingramcontent.com/pod-product-compliance
Lightning Source LLC
Chambersburg PA
CBHW081205170426
43197CB00018B/2928